Apple Training Series

A Teacher's Guide to Digital Media in the Classroom

Richard Harrington
with Ted Lai

Apple
Certified

Apple Training Series: A Teacher's Guide to Digital Media in the Classroom
Richard Harrington with Ted Lai
Copyright © 2009 by Peachpit Press

Published by Peachpit Press. For information on Peachpit Press books, contact:

Peachpit Press
1249 Eighth Street
Berkeley, CA 94710
(510) 524-2178
Fax: (510) 524-2221
http://www.peachpit.com
To report errors, please send a note to errata@peachpit.com
Peachpit Press is a division of Pearson Education

Apple Series Editor: Serena Herr
Project Editor: Serena Herr
Production Coordinator: Cory Borman
Proofer: Dave Awl
Compositor: Kate Kaminski, Happenstance Type-O-Rama
Indexer: Jack Lewis
Cover Illustration: Kent Oberheu
Cover Production: Happenstance Type-O-Rama

ISBN 10: 0-321-59143-7
ISBN 13: 978-0-321-59143-2
9 8 7 6 5 4 3 2 1
Printed and bound in the United States of America

Contents at a Glance

Foreword

In education and in technology, every moment is about change. By opening this book, you are asking questions about the risks and rewards of technological change in your classroom. It's the same question that teachers have been asking of themselves since the introduction of the Apple II computer in the early 80s. The one thing that's different is that, now more than ever, technology and digital media are everywhere. In fact, it's likely that you've picked up this book because you've seen your students' drive to express themselves outside of the classroom—on their cellphones, the internet, and through video sharing— become so pervasive that you want to channel that energy back into the classroom.

The Pearson Foundation launched the Digital Arts Alliance in 2005 with the aim of bringing the new world of digital arts directly to school classrooms. Since 2005, the growing alliance of public and private partnerships has delivered fully supported and staffed digital arts programs to more than 25,000 teachers and students internationally. Working together to design, develop, and complete digital projects tied to classroom objectives, students and educators achieve tangible results they can use immediately in their lives. The result is a new, 21st-century literacy—one that integrates core subject knowledge with learning and innovation skills; information, media, and technology skills; and essential life and career skills.

In the process, we've seen the impact that the latest digital hardware and software has on the way middle- and high-school students learn and share what they know. These new tools give young people the chance to develop and share their ideas in the same ways they communicate outside the classroom. More importantly, the polished video projects, websites, podcasts, video blogs, and DVDs they create with these tools give them the chance to makes their thoughts and ideas *part of the curriculum itself*, increasing their stake in their own learning, and in the learning of students, teachers, family, and friends outside the classroom.

Of all the changes the digital age has brought to learning, it's possible that greatest revolution will prove to be this one: students' ability to create work that, when completed, serves as a springboard for other students' explorations—expressing a feeling; making a factual or persuasive case; solving a problem; or telling a personal story.

We've seen first-hand that being able to create a final product that looks just like the pervasive information products that define their own culture makes it intrinsically more interesting for young people to learn the steps required to share their ideas. Students feel they have increased power to evaluate the result of their efforts, and they also better see a world in which the collaborative, team-based skills they develop can be extended beyond their school experience.

All of this happens when students and teachers have access to the latest digital technology, but the classroom projects that make use of this technology rely most heavily on writing, researching, and composition—skills that have been taught since formal education began.

In the pages that follow, Richard Harrington shows teachers how to integrate digital arts into their existing curriculum using iLife '08, iWork '08, and practical, step-by-step projects. The goal of this book is to introduce this amazing software in exactly the same way Digital Arts Alliance members have learned to introduce digital arts projects. The projects follow classroom-tested guidelines developed in accordance with the National Educational Technology Standards from among a broad range of Digital Arts Alliance programs.

At the beginning of every chapter, you'll also find inspirational profiles of successful digital media classroom projects around the world. The examples are extraordinary because they are so commonplace. In many ways, that is the message of this Teacher's Guide: that now is the perfect time to take up these tools and classroom strategies because it's easy to get going and the payoff is great. And the key to making this all happen is in your hands, with your students, in your classroom.

I invite you to visit www.pearsonfoundation.org and www.digitalartsalliance.org to learn more about how teachers everywhere are using these strategies in their classrooms. While you're there, I hope you'll also learn more about Digital Arts Alliance workshops designed expressly for teachers like you, and about the growing library of digital-arts materials available to you and your students.

—*Mark Nieker*
   President and Executive Director, The Pearson Foundation

Getting Started

Few forces are greater than the drive of young people to express themselves. Their thoughts, feelings, points of view—all these come alive as students begin to understand who they are. At the same time, few forces are more influential than the classroom teacher in helping young people make the most of that energy. Without the power of the young person and the teacher, without the school to provide an environment, and without a community to hear youth voices, technology loses its context and drive, becoming esoteric and often uninteresting.

For students, a digital arts project is exciting, not because of technology, but because the learning itself seems more relevant and powerful. *Relevant*, because young people already see the world as an integrated array of sound, images, and various media that the culture uses to express itself. Digital arts bring that kind of product into the classroom setting. *Powerful*, because young people can access and learn the tools of digital communication easily, and can reach across the globe farther and faster than ever before. Digital arts are there at a time when young people feel the greatest need to develop their own voice, to talk about their history and identity, to empathize with their subject, or to work in ways that they feel move them forward in life.

The important thing about digital arts for teachers is that these projects introduce a process that relies most heavily on methods teachers already know—writing, researching, and composing—but to greater effect. For every week or two that a class may need to spend learning the technology of a digital arts project, twice as much or more will go into non-technology-based work to create all the ideas, narrative, images, and sound for the digital story. If you know how to teach, you are closer than you may think to making digital arts a reality in your classroom.

How to Use this Book

This book can be used as both a source of ideas and a step-by-step introduction to the tools and techniques of teaching digital arts projects in the classroom. The book offers three ways to inspire and inform the professional educator: lessons, case studies, and essential tips.

Lesson Plans

To serve as a starting point, five lesson plans are offered that can be used in any classroom. While each lesson plan is formed around a particular subject (such as science or history), you can adapt them to your own subject area or classroom needs.

▸ **Lesson Goals.** Describes what should be accomplished during the lesson.

▶ **The Digital Pay-Off**

Most teachers don't pursue personal accolades. We don't enter teaching intending to be exalted as heroes. We teach students because we care about education, about schools, about kids. We believe that every child can achieve, and we live for those "A-hah" moments when students have that personal epiphany of what they're learning and why.

That said, it's wonderfully satisfying when parents, other teachers, or administrators visit the classroom, look around at the projects, and say, "I wish I were still in school!" This simple phrase communicates so many things. It means that an outsider approves of how we're teaching. They realize that what we're doing in the classroom is engaging, educational, and relevant. It means that we're making a difference.

In all my years of teaching, I never got that gratifying comment when I assigned a traditional book report. Name any typical classroom project: dioramas, models of missions or forts, research projects with comb binding. None of these projects, no matter how engaging, garnered the type of response that the technology-infused projects did.

Videos, podcasts, Keynote presentations, picture books, musical raps, websites, DVDs, brochures, posters, and photo essays were just some of the projects in my classroom that really made parents, teachers, and administrators stop and think about how schools need to teach our kids in the 21st century. They realized just how much fun and functional school could be if we just let it happen—and it's these adults who need convincing. The kids know.

What you hold in your hands is a guide to help you let go and begin developing 21st century learning in the classroom. Richard Harrington has authored a plethora of books, including *Apple Training Series: iWork '08* and *iLife '08*. This guide is a companion to those books, a structure for dozens of technology-infused lessons that will help any teacher design lessons that are rich with communication, collaboration, and creativity.

Try these lessons and join us on this mission of enhancing teaching and learning with technology. I hope you find this work inspiring, because I would like nothing better than to visit your class afterward and exclaim, "I wish I were still in school!"

—Ted Lai, Apple Distinguished Educator

▶ **Learning Objectives.** Describes what academic and technical skills can be strengthened through the exercise.

▶ **Project Requirements.** Lists the technology and equipment needs for the activity.

▶ **Assessment Guidelines.** Offers suggestions on how to evaluate the approach to the lesson.

▶ **Getting Started.** Describes the steps required to plan for the project in the lesson.

▶ **Introducing the Project.** Suggests how to present the activity to the class as well as model the desired results.

▶ **Creating the Project.** Presents an organized approach to the key steps in creating the project. Additionally, the major technical steps are outlined for each task.

▶ **Publishing the Project.** Specific instructions on how to publish the project are offered. Several mediums from video and websites, to presentations and reports, are shown throughout the lessons.

▶ **Assessing the Project.** Advice on evaluating student performance.

Cameos

As a source of inspiration, the book features cameo appearances by five successful digital media classroom projects around the world, conducted by the Digital Arts Alliance and developed in accordance with the National Educational Technology Standards council. These case studies showcase possibilities for enriching the classroom experience.

Essential Techniques

To help you get the most from iLife and iWork, we offer detailed instructions for five common tasks you'll need to perform in a classroom (and 15 more available online at the book's companion web page, www.peachpit.com/ats.teachersguide).

About the Apple Training Series

To get up to speed faster and gain a more comprehensive mastery of iLife and iWork, we recommend that you work through the *Apple Training Series: iLife '08 and iWork '08* books, published by Peachpit Press, which serve as companions to this guide.

The self-paced books, which include DVDs jam-packed with practical media files, take readers step-by-step through essential, real-life tasks. The books are both a self-paced learning tool and the official curriculum of the Apple Training and Certification Program, used by schools and training centers worldwide, and are ideal for users of all levels. You will find an offer for the discounted bundle at the back of this guide.

iLife and iWork Training and Certification

Apple offers Associate-level training and certification for the iLife and iWork product suites. Educators and students can earn certification to validate entry level skills (Apple Certified Associate), complementing the professional level skills (Apple Certified Pro) that are offered at our Apple Authorized Training Centers (AATCs).

The iLife '08 and iWork '08 courses are based on *Apple Training Series: iLife '08* by Michael Cohen, Jeff Bollow, and Richard Harrington, and *Apple Training Series; iWork '08* by Richard Harrington. The books include DVDs with all required media. Course descriptions appear at http://training.apple.com/training/.

By passing an Apple certification exam, students can distinguish themselves to colleges or prospective employers as skilled users of the chosen applications. Once you earn iLife '08 or iWork '08 Trainer status by passing the associated $150 online exams, you can offer certification to your students. If you feel that you need additional preparation before taking the trainer exam, you may want to attend a course at one of our AATCs. To find a course in your area, visit http://training.apple.com/schedule.

Both courses include an end-user exam, which earns either *Apple Certified Associate, iWork '08* or *Apple Certified Associate, iLife '08* certification. Your school can purchase exam codes for $45. Students who pass will receive a certificate and certification logos.

Once you pass the Trainer exam, information on how to purchase exam codes will appear in the results email. If you do not pass the exam, retake instructions will appear in the results email. For more information, email associatecertification@apple.com.

Resources for iLife and iWork

▶ **iLife Online Tutorials.** Visit www.apple.com/ilife/tutorials/.

▶ **iWork Online Tutorials.** Visit www.apple.com/iwork/tutorials/.

▶ **Apple Discussions.** A rich online community is available at discussions.apple.com. There are several groups for all of the iLife and iWork applications.

▶ **Apple Support Pages.** For technical support and articles, visit Apple's support website; www.apple.com/support/ilife/ and http://www.apple.com/support/iwork/.

▶ **Apple – Education.** The Apple website offers extensive case studies and educational resources. To browse offerings organized by grade level, visit www.apple.com/education/.

▶ **Apple Training Series books**. The official guides to both iLife and iWork offer hands on practice. Be sure to see the back of this book for discounted pricing offers.

1

Goals

Express a feeling through the use of words and images.

Create a slideshow and music to accompany the poem.

Present the poem and photos to the class in a multimedia performance.

Publish the poem and photos to the Internet.

Requirements

Recommended hardware and software:

▶ Macintosh computers

▶ Digital cameras

▶ Pages (part of iWork '08)

▶ iPhoto (part of iLife '08)

▶ iWeb (part of iLife '08)

▶ iTunes

▶ Web hosting service or account

Lesson 1

Express a Feeling or an Idea

One goal of any classroom is to help students learn to express their feelings and ideas. This expression can manifest itself in many ways, including poetry, art, photography, and music. Self-expression helps students develop a sense of self and improves their ability to communicate.

Digital tools have made it easier for many students to explore creative outlets. By using digital tools, students can craft their words, capture and manipulate images, add sound or music, and publish their thoughts to a global audience with ease.

Project Summary

As part of a lesson exploring visual literacy, students create a photo essay that expresses a feeling. Students use Pages as they write a short poem that expresses an emotion. The students then gather photographs or shoot digital photos to illustrate their poem. To organize and edit their images, students use iPhoto. The photo essays can then be shown in class with a slideshow as students read their poems. Lastly, the photo essay can be published to the Internet using iWeb.

Learning Objectives

After completing this project, students will be able to:

Academic

- ▶ Use creative writing to express a feeling or emotion that the student has experienced.
- ▶ Further visual literacy by gathering images or acquiring digital photos that support and enhance the written word.
- ▶ Analyze, edit, and arrange their images and words into a compelling form.
- ▶ Present their work both in person and on the Internet.

Technical

- ▶ Use Pages to write a poem.
- ▶ Import and organize digital images with iPhoto.
- ▶ Edit images with iPhoto by cropping or making adjustments that improve their clarity and impact.
- ▶ Add music to a slideshow with iTunes and iPhoto.
- ▶ Publish a web page with iWeb.

Assessment Guidelines

Student's Role

Students design their approach to the lesson, including the following.

- ▶ Decide on the feeling or emotion to express.

▶ Use the steps of the writing process to create a poem.

▶ Gather, edit, enhance, and organize images that support the words and emotions featured in the poem.

▶ Select music to use in the presentation that enhances the student's words and images.

▶ Arrange images and words on a web page, and publish it.

With the teacher's guidance, the students create a rubric to assess the success of the project.

TIP If you need help creating rubrics, try using Rubistar from www.4teachers.org. It's a free online rubric creator that supports multimedia projects.

Teacher's Role

Determine the criteria for evaluating student's work throughout the project. Explain how you will assess both the project itself and the student's technical skills, including:

▶ The use of the writing process for the creation of the student's poem.

▶ The selection or acquisition of digital images that support the student's poetry.

▶ The overall presentation of the poem and images through the student's public performance and slideshow.

▶ The ability of students to edit their digital images with iPhoto to improve image quality and appearance.

▶ The ability to select and arrange their images in a cohesive and influential manner using an iPhoto slideshow.

▶ The ability of the student to publish their work to the Internet as a web page.

Be sure to explain to students how you will evaluate their ability to reach the goals and objectives of the project, as judged by the final product.

Getting Started

Teacher Planning

In order for the lesson to succeed, you'll need a working knowledge of the technology and a general timeline for the project. You should:

- ▶ Understand the basic functionality of Pages, the word processing application included with iWork (see Lesson 7 of *Apple Training Series: iWork '08*).

- ▶ Understand the basic functionality of iPhoto, the digital imaging application included with iLife (see Lessons 1-4 of *Apple Training Series: iLife '08*).

- ▶ Familiarize yourself with the digital cameras available to students so you can answer their questions.

- ▶ Familiarize yourself with several websites that provide rights-free images for use in the project (if digital cameras are unavailable).

- ▶ Develop guidelines for the length and content of the student presentations.

- ▶ Ensure that the required hardware and software are available to the students.

- ▶ Determine the amount of time to be spent on the project, and provide suggested timeframes for project milestones. For example, how much time should the students spend gathering photos, or preparing the slideshow.

- ▶ You may also want to build a sample project that shows the intended results. This will help model the lesson and give you a chance to experience the technical requirements first hand.

Student Preparation

It's a good idea to give the students some time to experiment with the hardware and software they will use before they start the photo essay project. Ideally, before they start the project, let students:

- ▶ Explore Pages and use it as a word processing tool.

- ▶ Practice importing images into iPhoto and using tools to improve images. A useful practice exercise can be adapted from Lesson 1 of *Apple Training Series: iLife '08*.

- ▶ Explore the basics of creating web pages with iWeb. A practice exercise can be adapted from Lessons 14 and 15 of *Apple Training Series: iLife '08*.

Introducing the Project

- ▶ Successfully introducing the project is important to ensuring student success. The first step is to show some examples of good photo essays. There are numerous examples online; here are a few to start you off:

▶ **Time Magazine Photo Essays** – www.time.com/time/photoessays

▶ **UNICEF Photo Essays** – www.unicef.org/photoessays

▶ **The Photo Essay** – www.thephotoessay.com

Next, present the students with a list of possible themes for their poems. Depending on the subject of the course and age of the students, topics can be assigned or students can choose their own. Sample topics include:

▶ Describe an emotion you have felt recently.

▶ Choose a historical event and write a poem from the emotional perspective of one of the event's participants.

▶ Describe a color and its emotional impact.

▶ Select a scene or section from a core literature book and write a poem based on the emotions of one of the main characters.

The order in which the two primary tasks are completed for this lesson can vary based upon the students' strengths and interests. Some students will choose to first write their poem and then focus on selecting images that illustrate it. Other students may choose to use their own photographs, then write a poem that accompanies the images. This flexibility helps meet the needs of different learning styles and can result in a welcome variety of outcomes for the project.

Depending on the subject matter of the course and time allotted for the project, there's room for additional self-expression by the students. For example, students can choose to simply gather photos or to use a digital camera to take their own. Likewise, students may choose to use a pre-recorded song or experiment with the musical creation tools found in GarageBand.

> **NOTE** ▶ GarageBand is included in iLife '08 and offers numerous musical options. It includes several completed songs (called Jingles) as well as the ability to create original music using loops (samples) and software instruments or even record real instruments. With the Magic GarageBand feature, students can select a multi-track song from nine genres of music and change instruments and tempo to create their own interpretation of the musical selection. For an introduction to GarageBand, see Lesson 13 in *Apple Training Series iLife '08*.

Small is Beautiful

Crater High School, Oregon

IN THE 1980S AND 1990S, OREGON'S CRATER HIGH School received widespread recognition for its innovation in establishing four excellent small schools within a school. Today, this school of more than 1,500 students, which serves the rural communities of Central Point and Gold Hill, is reinvigorated, putting renewed focus on smaller, more personalized, and more rigorous schools with the support of E3's Oregon Small Schools Initiative.

As part of the redesign initiative, lead teachers from each of Crater's four new schools–the School of Business Innovation & Science (BIS), the Renaissance Academy, the Academy of Health and Public Service, and the Academy of Natural Science–participated in a digital storytelling workshop supported by E3 and the Pearson Foundation.

To develop their digital stories, student participants worked in teams, first collaborating to convert their research into scripts they recorded as voiceover tracks. Next, they sourced relevant digital imagery to illustrate specific details and perspectives concerning their chosen topics. Finally, they created titles, worked with transitions, chose music to set the appropriate tone, and experimented with special effects to complete their films.

Here are some examples of Crater High teachers using digital arts to support poetry, English, and foreign language instruction:

I Have a Dream
Using the text of Harper Lee's *To Kill a Mockingbird* and Martin Luther King, Jr.'s "I have a dream" speech as a launching point, Ms. James's sophomore Integrated English and History students explored the efforts of African Americans to achieve equality during the Civil Rights Movement.

Synthesizing what they learned about discrimination, participating students were encouraged to apply their knowledge by demonstrating how a contemporary minority group or portion of the population in America today continues the struggle to achieve equality (http://pearsonfoundation-e3.org/ds/craterhs07/James/index.htm).

Hablo, Hablas, Hablan

Ms. Rogers used a digital storytelling project in her Spanish II class to support both review and expansion of Spanish grammar and vocabulary, as well as students' written and oral proficiencies. With the guideline that they should choose subjects for their stories that would enhance their exposure to Spanish and Latino culture, students were allowed to select their own topics.

After the students conducted their research, they were encouraged to explore the use of various verb tenses (present, imperfect, preterit, gerund, past perfect) as they collaborated in pairs to create the scripts for their digital stories (short films). This process focused learning by facilitating student interaction with native Spanish-speakers of varying ages and backgrounds; increasing students' confidence in using language appropriate to particular social contexts; and, finally, helping students to function in Spanish with increasing ease (http://pearsonfoundation-e3.org/ds/craterhs07/Rogers/index.htm).

Speak the Speech, I Prithee

Ms. Palmer's Shakespeare class used digital storytelling as the culminating project for a unit that also required research papers exploring the fifteenth and sixteenth centuries. To provide a clear context for Shakespeare's work, and to gain a better understanding of what it must have been like to live during Shakespearean times, the students' research papers focused on some of the people, events, and practices that defined Renaissance life (http://pearsonfoundation-e3.org/ds/craterhs07/Palmer/index.htm).

Creating the Project

This project can be broken into several tasks, which you can adapt as needed to meet the educational goals and time constraints of your classroom, as well as the age and ability levels of your individual students.

Write a Poem

After you have introduced the themes as discussed above, give the students time to write their poems. Some may choose to work with pen and paper, others will be more comfortable typing as they create. In either case, the students will eventually need to enter their poems using the Pages word processing application to transfer the text to a variety of digital projects.

1 Launch the Pages application.

   Depending on your computer's setup, you'll find Pages located either in the computer's Dock or by navigating to the iWork folder inside your Applications folder.

2 From the Template Chooser, select the Blank template and click Choose. A new, blank document opens.

3 Type your poem using standard word processing functions.

> **TIP** ▶ Students can use several tools to assist with their writing. Simply highlight a word and choose Edit > Writing Tools > Look Up in Dictionary or Thesaurus. Students can also access Google and Wikipedia searches from the same menu.

4 Use standard formatting commands by accessing the Format Bar at the top of the document window.

5 Choose Edit > Spelling > Check Spelling to check your document for spelling and grammar errors.

6 Throughout the writing process, choose File > Save to capture your writing.

Students should store their work in a folder on the computer for the assignment.

7 To print a document, choose File > Print and select a printer on your classroom network.

> **MORE INFO** ▶ The word processing features of Pages are covered in Lesson 7 of *Apple Training Series iWork '08*.

Capture or Gather Digital Images

Students will need images or photos to complete their photo essay. The approach taken here will vary based upon access to digital cameras and time allowed.

▶ Students can use digital cameras to take their own photos. Encourage students to capture images that complement their words and have visual impact. This task is open to great amounts of self-expression.

▶ Students can use the built-in iSight camera and Photobooth software on their Mac to capture images. This option works well for portraits or items that can be held in front of the computer.

iStockphoto/VikramRaghuvanshi

▶ Students can search for appropriate, copyright-friendly images on the Internet. Be sure to harness the SafeSearch filters of Google Image Search or access other appropriate web engines to look for photos. Be sure to have students properly cite photo credits of their selected images.

NOTE ▶ There are a number of Internet sites with copyright-friendly images, including www.pics4learning.com and www.kitzu.org. Educational sites like these are focused on providing students and educators with high-quality images without copyright or royalty concerns. Google Image Searches are convenient, but may be subject to copyright restrictions if students are posting their work online or entering it into contests.

▶ Students can use scanners to import printed images into a computer.

▶ Students can bring in their own personal digital photos.

In all cases, have the students save their images into an individual folder within their project folder.

Organize Digital Images

It's likely that students will collect more images than they need for the project. An important part of the process of making a photo essay is sorting through the gathered images, selecting only the best to use, and then arranging those into an order that supports the student's writing.

1   Launch the iPhoto application by clicking its icon in the computer's Dock.

2   Choose File > Import to Library to add the students' images to the iPhoto library. A file navigation window opens.

3   Have the students navigate to their images folder, and click Import.

iPhoto imports each image and displays the photo as it imports. The images are added to iPhoto and the Last Import button is selected.

NOTE ▸ You can also drag a group of photos onto the iPhoto icon in your dock. The images will be imported in a similar fashion.

4   Double-click the Event name and make sure that Event matches the title of the student's poem. This will make it easier to find the images.

Images can be sorted to make it easier to select the best images.

5   Double-click the Event to open it.

6   Choose View > Rating to add star ratings to the images.

This ranking process helps students to evaluate their images and choose the best ones for the photo essay.

7   Evaluate each image, then assign a one-, two-, three-, four-, or five-star rating to each.

Stars can be assigned by clicking the circles below each image or by pressing Command + 1–5 (for 1–5 stars respectively).

8   To see only the best images first, choose View > Sort Photos > By Rating, then Choose View > Sort Photos > Descending.

9   Hide any photos you don't want to use by first clicking an image once and then choosing Photos > Hide Photo (or pressing Command + L).

> **NOTE** ▶ Hidden photos are not deleted, merely hidden from view. A student can choose View > Hidden Photos to see any hidden images. Hiding images is part of the sorting process that is required to edit a photo essay.

Edit Digital Images

Once the students have selected their images, they can make additional edits to improve them. iPhoto supports many options to improve the appearance of photos.

1   To edit an image, select its thumbnail and click the Edit button.

iPhoto's viewing pane becomes a picture-editing pane. A collection of editing tools appears below the image.

2   Select from the many tools in the toolbar.

▶   **Rotate** – Allows you to rotate an image 90° counter-clockwise. By holding the Option key while clicking, the image will rotate 90° clockwise instead.

▶   **Crop** – Allows you to remove distracting parts of an image or to improve the overall composition. Be sure to explore the Constrain option if you want to resize the image for the computer monitor or another output format.

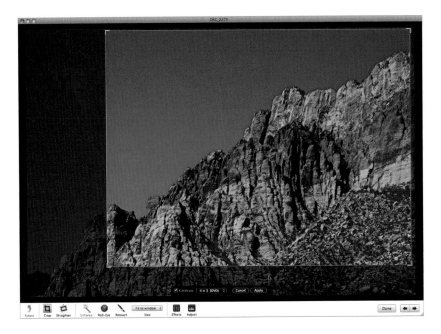

▶ **Straighten** – This command compensates for photos taken at an angle.

▶ **Enhance** – This command brightens the photo or adjusts contrast levels based on preset criteria.

▶ **Red-Eye** – This fixes red-eye in an image caused by flash photography in low-light situations.

▶ **Retouch** – Allows for the removal of skin and other blemishes by blending them into the background.

▶ **Effects** – iPhoto offers several effects including turning a color photo into black and white, adding a vignette, or giving it a sepia tone.

▶ **Adjust** – iPhoto offers precise control with advanced editing commands. The student can address issues like exposure and contrast, color saturation, sharpness, noise reduction, and color balance.

MORE INFO ▶ For a detailed explanation of most of the image-editing tools, be sure to see Lesson 3 of *Apple Training Series: iLife '08*. You can also choose Help > Video Tutorials to see instruction on several of the commands.

3   When you've finished editing the image, click the arrow buttons to navigate to additional images or the Done button to close the editing pane.

> **NOTE** ▸ If you want to remove all changes to an image, you can easily revert to the original by navigating to Photos > Revert to Original.

Create a Slideshow with Music

Once the images are selected and edited, students will create a slideshow to display their images. Slideshows can display images for different lengths of time as well as use music for accompaniment. In order to time their slideshows accurately, students should read their poems aloud and determine the timing for each image.

1   With the student's Event still open, click the + segment in the multi-segment button at the bottom of the source list.

2   In the sheet that appears, click the Slideshow button, name the Slideshow, and then click Create.

A slideshow heading appears in the source list and the slideshow editing area opens.

3 In the toolbar at the bottom of the slideshow editing area, click the Settings button.

A sheet appears with options for modifying the slideshow.

4 Make sure the Repeat slideshow checkbox is deselected.

5 Click the Music button in the toolbar to select a song to use. A sheet appears prompting the student to select a song from either iTunes or GarageBand.

MORE INFO ▶ You can find more out about using GarageBand to create music by reading Lessons 11 & 13 of *Apple Training Series iLife '08*. For more on iTunes, see www.apple.com/itunes/tutorials.

6 Select a music track and click OK.

NOTE ▶ Students should be encouraged to use instrumental music that does not have lyrics that compete with their voice or change the meaning of their poetry.

7 Drag the images into their desired order in the sorting area.

If the student decides to remove an image from their slideshow, just press the Delete key.

8   Click the Adjust button in the toolbar to set the duration for each slide. You can also choose a Transition between this image and the next.

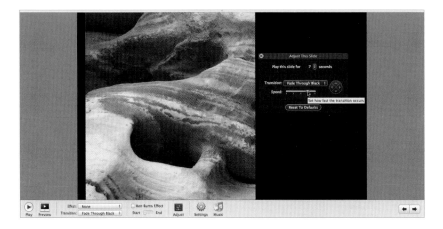

MORE INFO ▶ You can find more out about creating slideshows by reading Lesson 4 of the Apple Training Series: iLife '08 book.

9   Click the Play button and rehearse your presentation.

Publishing the Project

Once the student has completed their slideshow and poem, they should rehearse their presentations for performing in front of the class. Students do not need to memorize their poems, but should feel comfortable reading their poetry while using the music and images of their slideshow as background material. Students should be encouraged to rehearse their poem so that they sound like they are *speaking* instead of *reading*. Learning how to use their voice effectively with inflection is an essential tool in compelling communication.

Publish as a Slideshow Movie

To make it easier to play all of the slideshows from a single computer in the classroom, students should publish their slideshows as movie files. Each student will need to do this from the computer on which they originally built their slideshow.

1   With the slideshow open, choose File > Export. A sheet appears asking you to name the movie and specify a location.

2   In the Save As field, name the movie with your first and last name, then specify a location to save the file.

Save As: Maya Mulligrew

Where: Movies

Movie size: Large (640x480)

Cancel   Export

3   Choose a size from the sheet's "Movie size" pop-up menu.

Larger movies will look much better when presented on a large screen, but will require more disk space to store.

4   Click the Export button to write the file to disk.

5   When finished, copy files to a central computer attached to a projector for playback in the classroom.

Make sure the computer has speakers attached so the sound can be clearly heard. Let students adjust their playback volume, but be sure the music doesn't overpower their voices.

Publish as a Web Page

Sharing images via the Internet has become a popular form of communication in the modern age. This task of the project is optional, but is an excellent way for students to share their work, explore visual and media literacy, and learn more about publishing.

> **NOTE** ▶ If the students are not using their own images for the photo essay, be sure they properly cite their sources and that the project is for academic purposes.

Sending photos to the web is very easy with iWeb. It will require that your school have a web-hosting space configured, however, so be sure to check with your school's technology department.

1   In the Sources list on the student's computer, have them click Events and then select their photos in the Event list.

2   Choose Share > Send to iWeb > Photo Page.

Depending upon your school's security and network settings, some dialog boxes may appear asking permission to access your image library and network.

3   iWeb launches and offers several different styles of templates.

4   Pick a template that matches the style of your photo and then click Choose.

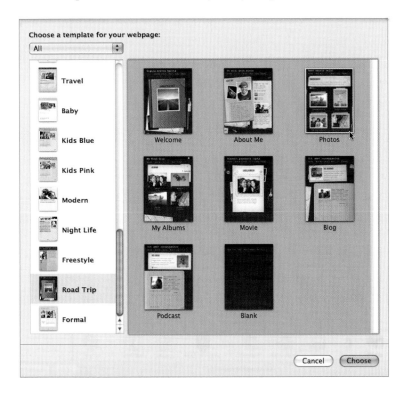

5   In the Photo Grid inspector adjust the number of columns to 1 or 2, and set the size of the Caption lines to accommodate the text of the poem.

6   Drag the photos to rearrange their order.

7   Type captions, or copy and paste them from the Pages document into iWeb.

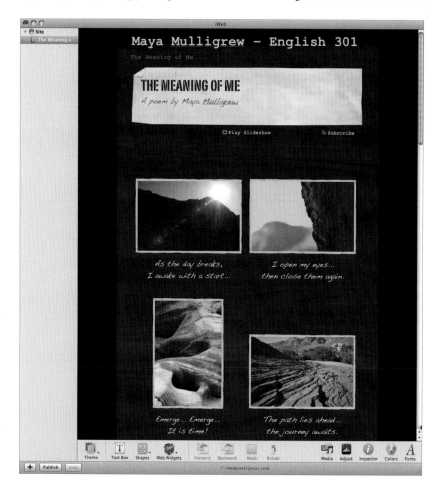

8   When finished, click the Publish button to post the web page.

>   **MORE INFO** ▶ You can find more out about creating web pages in Lessons 14 and 15 of *Apple Training Series iLife '08*.

Assessing the Project

There are several ways to evaluate the student's performance for the lesson. Be sure to evaluate all aspects of the project, looking at the creativity and effectiveness of the photo essay, as well as the technical performance of the tasks.

▶   Students should submit their poems in printed form and include any drafts and revisions for evaluation. These can be graded using standard practices for creative writing.

▶   Assess the students' performance of their photo essay slideshow. Be sure to keep in mind any state standards on speaking and incorporate opportunities for peer review.

▶   Invite discussion, journal entries, or other follow-up activities regarding the project.

▶   Have students complete self-assessment rubrics to justify their achievements in expressing a feeling.

2

Goals

Evaluate the question: "Does the presence of road salt affect plant growth?"

Form an initial hypothesis to the question.

Design an experiment to test the hypothesis.

Collect and analyze data from the experiment.

Formulate a conclusion.

Present the findings and conclusion to the class.

Requirements

Recommended hardware and software:

▶ Macintosh computers

▶ Digital cameras

▶ Numbers (part of iWork '08)

▶ Keynote (part of iWork '08)

Recommended equipment for the experiment:

▶ Plant seeds

▶ Road salt

▶ 5 oz. planting pots

▶ Potting soil

▶ Rulers

Make a Case: Factual Presentations

Teaching students how to research a problem, develop a theory, test the theory, reach a conclusion, and make a case defending the conclusion is often referred to as teaching the scientific method, yet it has many applications. Students need to learn how to devise possible solutions to a problem in all disciplines, and then test the solutions to determine the best approach.

The use of digital tools can make it easier for students to collect and analyze data. Students can then effectively present and communicate their findings using charts and images as reinforcement.

Project Summary

This project is designed to teach students how to use scientific observation to test a theory. In this example, students test to see if the presence of road salt affects plant growth. Students work in collaborative learning groups and track their observations using a spreadsheet in Numbers. They also gather photographic data of the results at predetermined milestones throughout the experiment, as evidence of their findings. Students then analyze their data and reach a conclusion. Finally, students create a presentation, using Keynote, to communicate their findings to the class.

Learning Objectives

After completing this project, students will be able to:

Academic

▶ Use the scientific method to evaluate a problem and devise possible outcomes.

▶ Collect and analyze data over an extended period of time.

▶ Present their conclusions orally, using visual reinforcement.

Technical

▶ Use Numbers to organize, analyze, and represent data.

▶ Capture digital images of the experiment.

▶ Organize digital images of the experiment with iPhoto.

▶ Build a presentation using Keynote.

▶ Print their findings and presentation for grading.

Assessment Guidelines

Student's Role

Students design their approach to the lesson, including the following:

▶ Forming a hypothesis.

▶ Performing experiments.

▶ Determining how much data to collect.

▶ Collecting images that support their conclusion.

▶ Creating a slide presentation to help them communicate their results.

With the teacher's guidance, the students should create a rubric to assess the outcomes of the project.

> **TIP** ▶ If you need help creating rubrics, you can use Rubistar from www.4teachers.org. It's a free online rubric creator that supports multimedia projects.

Teacher's Role

Determine the criteria for evaluating the student's work throughout the project and explain how you will assess the parts of the project, including:

▶ The accurate collection of data.

▶ The conclusion reached by the student.

▶ The overall presentation of the groups findings.

Establish and explain the criteria that will be used for evaluating the student's technical skills, including:

▶ The use of a spreadsheet to input and evaluate data.

▶ The use of digital photos and measurement to record data.

▶ The ability to select and arrange images and charts into a comprehensive and effective Keynote presentation.

Be sure to explain to students how you will evaluate their ability to reach the goals and objectives of the project, as judged by the final product.

Getting Started

Teacher Planning

In order for the lesson to succeed, you will need a working knowledge of the technology, including:

▶ The basic functionality of Numbers, the spreadsheet application included with iWork (see Lessons 10 & 11 of *Apple Training Series: iWork '08*).

▶ The basic functionality of iPhoto, the digital imaging application included with iLife (see Lessons 1-4 of *Apple Training Series: iLife '08*).

▶ The basic functionality of Keynote, the presentation application included with iWork (see Lesson 1-4 of *Apple Training Series: iWork '08*).

▶ Familiarity with the digital cameras available to students, so you can answer questions.

▶ Ensure that the required hardware and software are available to the students.

▶ Develop guidelines for the length of the experiment and frequency of measurement.

Student Preparation

This project requires little experience to get started, in that the data collection and entry tasks are easily learned. What may take some time is learning how to build a presentation using Keynote.

▶ Students can begin to use Numbers right away, as a Science Lab template is pre-built and easy to use. Students should be familiar with how the individual sheets and tables in the Science Lab template are linked.

▶ Students can practice importing images into iPhoto and organizing them. A useful practice exercise can be adapted from Lesson 1 of *Apple Training Series: iLife '08*.

▶ Students can practice using Keynote to build a presentation by creating sample charts and using the Media Browser to add photos to slides.

Introducing the Project

Organize the students into small groups for the exercise (existing lab groups will also work). A group of three to four students is the right size and will help facilitate active participation by all members.

Next, pose the question: "Does the presence of road salt affect plant growth?" Inform students that they should develop an initial answer to the question based on their expectations.

Present the students with the following items:

▶ Plant seeds

▶ Road salt

▶ Generic fertilizer

▶ 5 oz. planting pots

▶ Potting soil

Planning the Project

Over the course of approximately 15 weeks, students will track the growth of two groups of plants. One group will be exposed to a specified amount of road salt, while the other group will serve as a control group. Students should keep all other variables (light, water, airflow, and so forth) the same for both groups.

> **NOTE** ▶ Although a 15-week period is called for in the Numbers template, the exact duration of the experiment can be set to meet your classroom needs.

Creating the Project

This experiment takes several weeks to complete as it requires that the plants have time to grow (and react) in their tested conditions. As such, the lesson should be spread out over a semester.

Develop the Experiment

Present the students with their experiment materials and the timeframe for their experiment. Give them 15 minutes to design an experiment that would allow them to test their hypothesis. After the specified design time, have a group discussion with the class to create the testing scenario.

> **NOTE** ▶ Although this lesson identifies a general experiment approach, you are encouraged to adapt this lesson to match your needs and your students' ideas. One goal here is to encourage students to develop their own way of making a case.

Build the Experiment

Have students place the potting soil and fertilizer into the planting pots. Be sure that they add the same amounts and mixture to each pot. Students then place seeds into each pot and add water. The pots should be placed in an area with sunlight and allowed to grow.

Have students number the pots so they can be consistently tracked. It is suggested that you use 10 pots in the control group and 10 pots in the test group. To the test group, add a small amount of road salt (using the same amount for each test item). Water the plants each week and add the identical small amount (a few grains) of road salt each week.

Body of Knowledge

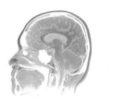

FROM ELEMENTARY SCHOOL THROUGH COLLEGE, education is at once about learning a subject and about learning how to learn. This is especially true in science. Many aspects of science involve the ability of the student to make sense of large bodies of information and how those elements work together in a common discipline. Disciplines like biology and environmental science, meanwhile, are wholly synthetic, integrating many intellectual areas external to the conventional scientific method.

Successful science students learn how to make sense out of a huge volume of information and how to organize it all in a way that is comprehensible. This is true from basic projects like weather and climate investigations in middle school through advanced undergraduate college classes. In the Digital Arts Alliance, whether dealing with basic principles or the intricacies of biology, anatomy and physiology, and chemistry, digital arts give students a framework to integrate what they know in a way that grabs other students' attention.

One example is the projects that students created in Ms. Veghin-Johnson's fifth-grade class at New York City's P.S. 146 during the 2005–06 school year. This class produced digital stories on key systems and parts of the human body. Working in teams, the students researched their subjects and wrote detailed scripts based on their findings. To see examples of their work, visit www.digitalartsalliance.org/partnerships/mli.

Present the Problem

Divide the students into lab groups to perform the experiment. Present the question "Does the presence of road salt affect plant growth?" Give the students 15 minutes to discuss the question and write down their initial hypothesis.

Develop the Experiment

Present the students with their experiment materials and the timeframe for their experiment. Give them 15 minutes to design an experiment that would allow them to test their hypothesis. After the specified design time, have a group discussion with the class to create the testing scenario.

> **NOTE** ▶ Although this lesson identifies a general experiment approach, you are encouraged to adapt this lesson to match your needs and your students' ideas. One goal here is to encourage students to develop their own way of making a case.

Build the Experiment

Have students place the potting soil and fertilizer into the planting pots. Be sure that they add the same amounts and mixture to each pot. Students then place seeds into each pot and add water. The pots should be placed in an area with sunlight and allowed to grow.

Have students number the pots so they can be consistently tracked. It is suggested that you use 10 pots in the control group and 10 pots in the test group. To the test group, add a small amount of road salt (using the same amount for each test item). Water the plants each week and add the identical small amount (a few grains) of road salt each week.

Measure the Results

Students should take measurements of each plant at predetermined regular intervals (such as every two weeks). The goal is to measure the height of the plant. Students should use both rulers to measure growth in centimeters as well as capture photographic evidence of the plant growth. Students can also be encouraged to gather photographic evidence, placing a measurement tool beside the plant to show the growth. The measurement data should be logged into a Numbers spreadsheet.

1   Launch the Numbers application.

Depending on your computer's setup, you'll either find Numbers located in the computer's Dock or by navigating to the iWork folder inside your Applications folder.

2   From the Template Chooser select the Education category, then the Science Lab template, and click Choose.

A new document opens. This is a worksheet that can be used as is or that can be adapted to work for the students' exercise.

NOTE ► Be sure to emphasize to the students that the data and results listed in the spreadsheet are placeholder data and meant to be illustrative. Be clear that the results they capture will differ from the results in the template and they will enter their own data throughout the 15 weeks.

3   In the text block on the first sheet, have students enter their own hypothesis, materials list, and procedure description.

4   Have them erase the conclusion listed, as they'll need to generate their own.

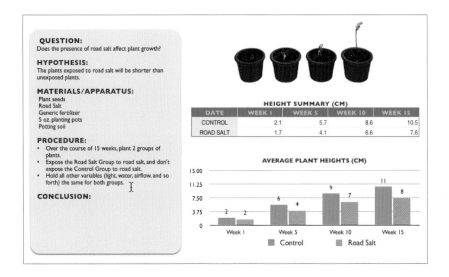

5 In the Sheets list, click the Lab Worksheet to switch sheets.

6 In the Control Group table, have students select the cells containing the weekly measurements (Cells B2–E11).

7 Erase the sample data by pressing the Delete key.

PLANT	WEEK 1	WEEK 5	WEEK 10	WEEK 15		PLANT	WEEK 1	WEEK 5	WEEK 10	WEEK 15
1						1	1.60	4.40	7.00	7.60
2						2	1.40	4.20	6.60	7.10
3						3	1.70	4.80	6.80	7.40
4						4	2.00	5.00	7.50	8.60
5						5	1.50	3.80	6.00	7.30
6						6	1.70	3.90	6.40	7.60
7						7	1.80	4.00	6.90	8.60
8						8	2.00	4.20	6.60	7.30
9						9	1.70	3.00	5.50	6.80
10						10	1.90	3.90	6.30	7.60
Average	▲	▲	▲	▲		Average	1.73	4.12	6.56	7.59

NOTE ▶ Make sure students do not erase the formulas contained at the bottom of the table that average the data for each week.

8   Repeat the clearing of data for the Road Salt table.

9   Have students enter their data for the height of each plant.

Use a decimal-based approach, for example 10.50 for a plant that is 10 and one half centimeters tall.

CONTROL GROUP				
PLANT	WEEK 1	WEEK 5	WEEK 10	WEEK 15
1	1.20			
2	1.10			
3	1.20			
4	1.30			
5	1.25			
6	1.15			
7	1.10			
8	1.00			
9	1.25			
10	1.30			
Average	1.19	▲	▲	▲

	A	B	C	D	E
	PLANT	WEEK 1	WEEK 5	WEEK 10	WEEK 15
1		ROAD SALT			
2	1	1.10			
3	2	1.00			
4	3	0.95			
5	4	1.20			
6	5	1.15			
7	6	1.05			
8	7	1.10			
9	8	1.20			
10	9	1.25			
11	10	1.15			
12	Average	1.12	▲	▲	▲

10 After the data is entered for the observation period, be sure students save their work.

TIP ▶ Because the experiment runs over several weeks, students should back up their data. This could mean copying the file to a storage device, such as a key drive or hard drive, as well as making interim printouts of their worksheet.

MORE INFO ▶ The spreadsheet features of Numbers are covered in Lesson 10 of the Apple Training Series iWork '08 book.

Capture Digital Photos

Students will need photos to document their experiment. High quality cameras are not needed, but the number of each plant and its group designation should be clearly visible in the image. Students should attempt to frame the images in a consistent way so that accurate changes can be captured.

NOTE ▶ If the classroom doesn't have enough digital cameras, students can use an iSight camera and Photo Booth to take images of their plant. Initially, the resulting photo will be a mirror image, but you can choose Edit > Flip photo to get a proper photo.

Organize Digital Images

Students can use iPhoto to organize their digital images. iPhoto will automatically add date information that will make it easy to organize the students' photographic evidence.

1   Launch the iPhoto application by clicking its icon in the computer's Dock.

2   Students should plug the camera in to their computer with a USB cable, then power it on.

3   Once the camera is connected and iPhoto detects it, iPhoto switches to an import view and the camera appears in the Source list.

> **TIP** ▶ If iPhoto does not recognize your camera, check the cable connection and make sure the camera is powered on. Your camera must be set to its correct mode to transfer images (see the instructions provided with your camera or check with your school's technology group).

4   Students should type an Event name for the group of photos they are importing. They can add important information in the Description area (for example, whether this is a control or test group).

iPhoto will group the imported photos using this name in the library.

5   Students should type a description for the photos in the Description field.

This description should include the date information, as well as the students' group name.

> **TIP** ▶ To import only some of the photos on the camera, select only the photos needed. Do this by Command-clicking each thumbnail, or drag to select a set of photos. If there are photos still on the camera that were already imported, hide them from the import view by selecting "Hide photos already imported."

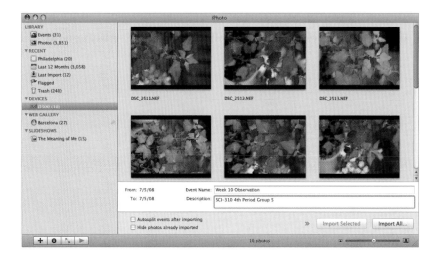

6   Click the Import All button to import the photos from the camera.

iPhoto will ask you if you want to delete photos once they have been imported. This is usually the right choice as it frees up space on the camera. To cancel photo transfer, simply click Stop Import.

7   When all of the photos have been transferred, the camera can be ejected and disconnected.

Complete the Experiment

Once the data has been captured for the required length of the experiment, the Numbers Lab Experiment template will create visual representations to help the students evaluate their data.

▶   On the Lab Worksheet students will find both a table and a chart. Both show the distribution of the plant heights by frequency.

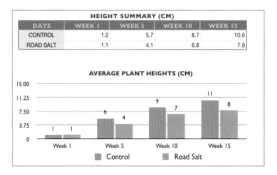

▶ On the Summary sheet, students can analyze another table and chart. These both show the average plant height in each group, broken down by measurement interval.

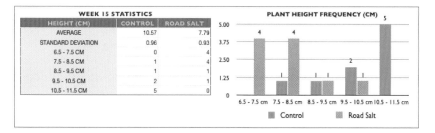

After analyzing their data, the groups should write a conclusion that summarizes their findings. Students should base their conclusions on the data they observed and they should be encouraged to include vocabulary and ideas that they have learned in class on this topic. Have students print their worksheet for submission by choosing File > Print.

Publishing the Project

Once the student group has completed their research, they should prepare a presentation to communicate their findings. Keynote makes it easy to create clear, multimedia-rich slides and integrates very well with Numbers and iPhoto (as well as the entire iWork and iLife suites). Students should keep their presentations short and to the point, using approximately 5-10 slides to make their case.

Creating the Presentation

The first task is to launch Keynote and select a theme for the presentation.

1   Launch the Keynote application.

Depending on your computer's setup, you'll find Keynote located either in the computer's Dock or by navigating to the iWork folder inside your Applications folder.

2 From the Theme chooser, pick a theme design that matches the group's desired look and click Choose.

A new presentation is created based upon the selected theme.

3 The students should create a title slate by modifying the text on slide 1.

Adding Additional Slides

Once a theme is selected, the students will need to add additional slides to their presentation. Fortunately, Keynote offers several preset layouts that match specific purposes (like displaying photos or showing bulleted text).

1 To add additional slides, click the New button in the toolbar.

2   To change the layout of a slide, select it in the Slides sorter, and then click the Masters button in the toolbar.

3   Pick a layout to match the purpose of the slide.

The Blank or Title - Top layouts work well to show charts.

The Photo layouts are an easy way to showcase photographic evidence.

4   As students add their information to the Keynote slides, remind them to keep the information simple. The Keynote presentation is a summary of the important steps and conclusion in their experiment. When they present in front of the class, they will explain things verbally in greater detail.

   MORE INFO ▶ You can find more out about creating presentations by reading Lessons 1 - 6 of the Apple Training Series iWork '08 book.

Using Information from Numbers

Most of the information for the presentation can come right from the students' worksheet in Numbers. iWork makes it easy to copy and paste information between applications.

1   To switch back to Numbers, click its icon in the Dock.

   NOTE ▶ If you don't see the Worksheet, click the Window menu and select it.

2   Select a table or chart by clicking its icon in the Sheets list.

3   Choose Edit > Copy.

4   Switch back to Keynote by clicking its icon in the Dock.

5   Select a slide in the Slides Navigator where you want the table or chart to be.

6   Click within the slide and choose Edit > Paste.

7   Scale the pasted content by dragging its corner handles.

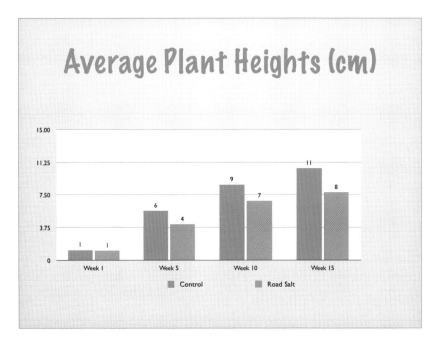

Using Photos from iPhoto
When working with Keynote, you can easily access any photos, movies, or audio clips by using the Media Browser. In fact, you can see all of the content from your iLife creations and most of the User folder in one convenient browser.

1   In the toolbar, click the Media button to open the Media Browser.

2   Choose Photos and click the iPhoto icon.

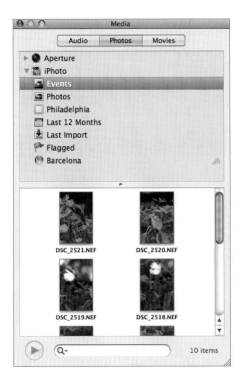

The contents of your iPhoto library will be displayed in the browser (if needed click the triangle to reveal the contents of your iPhoto library). Select the Events button and find the specific Event that contains the images of your plants.

3   Drag any photo from the Media Browser and drop it on to a slide or into an Object Placeholder.

The photo is added to your slide. If you need to resize an image, it is easy.

4   Click the Edit Mask button, then drag the corners of the photo or the slider to resize it.

When finished, click the Edit Mask button again.

Giving the Presentation

Students should properly save their presentation and rehearse it before delivering. Remind students that a presentation is where they explain everything they did and learned during the experiment or project. The Slides are merely summary notes to focus ideas and help them recall important data and information.

1   Choose File > Save and specify a location on the computer's hard drive or network.

2   Select the first slide and click the Play button in the toolbar to view all the slides.

The presentation enters a full-screen view.

3   Press the spacebar or Right Arrow key to advance the presentation.

4   When finished, press the Escape key to exit the presentation.

> **NOTE** ▶ Students can choose File > Record Slideshow to capture their presentation. This recording can then be turned into a podcast or a DVD. For more information see *Apple Training Series: iWork '08*.

Assessing the Project

There are several ways to evaluate the student's performance for the lesson. Be sure to evaluate all aspects of the project, looking at the testing and problem-solving process, as well as the technical proficiency in presenting their information and making a case.

▶   Students should submit their worksheets in printed form by choosing File > Print. Alternatively, if the teacher has a digital drop box set up, students can submit their work by choosing File > Export, creating a PDF of their presentation, and sending it to their instructor.

▶   Assess the students' ability to gather accurate data and photos for making their case.

▶   Evaluate the effectiveness and design of the group's presentation slides.

▶   Invite discussion, journal entries, or other follow-up activities regarding the project.

▶   Have students complete self-assessment rubrics to justify their success in making a case.

3

Goals

Make a persuasive case that clearly states a position and reinforces it for the audience with multiple relevant points.

Develop the argument and corresponding script to effectively communicate the group's position on a chosen topic.

Capture footage or photos as a group that can visually strengthen the argument.

Edit the elements together to create a television commercial or public service announcement.

Publish the commercial to a DVD for playback.

Requirements

Recommended hardware and software:

► Macintosh computers

► Digital video or photo cameras

► Numbers (part of iWork '08)

► Pages (part of iWork '08)

► iMovie (part of iLife '08)

► GarageBand (part of iLife '08)

► iDVD (part of iLife '08)

► DVD player or computer with DVD drive for playback

Make a Case: Persuasive Presentations

Students need to learn how to make persuasive presentations in order to present their ideas effectively. Whether the final product is an oral presentation accompanied by slides, a full-fleged edited video that reinforces the student's position with visuals, or anything in between, the ability to clearly present an opinion and influence an audience is an important life and career skill.

The use of digital tools has made it easier for many students to present their ideas in a way that emphasizes visual and media literacy. By using digital tools, students can organize their ideas, capture audio and video that reinforces their point, edit their material to refine the message, and publish their presentation to share it with ease.

Project Summary

As part of a lesson in history, social studies, science, or public speaking, students produce a television commercial or public service announcement to make a case to the viewing audience. Teachers can present a wide range of topics including past presidential campaigns, constitutional amendments, social issues, or scientific discoveries.

Students use Numbers to brainstorm, develop, and organize their argument. Next, the students use the writing process and Pages to create a script that makes a concise but effective case. The students then gather images using video or still photo cameras, and edit them together using iMovie. To create a polished presentation, students add music and sound effects using GarageBand. Lastly, the commercial can be published to disc using iDVD for playback on televisions or computers.

Learning Objectives

After completing this project, students will be able to:

Academic

▶   Develop and organize their thoughts to make a case.

▶   Use creative writing to express an opinion.

▶   Develop their visual literacy by gathering video or images that support the written word.

▶   Edit and arrange their images and words into a compelling form.

▶   Work in a collaborative group setting, delegating and sharing responsibilities to successfully complete the project.

Technical

▶   Use Numbers to capture and organize persuasive arguments.

▶   Use Pages to write a script for the television commercial.

▶   Shoot video footage or acquire digital photos.

▶   Edit their footage or images together using iMovie.

▶   Add music and sound effects with GarageBand.

▶   Publish a DVD with iDVD.

Assessment Guidelines

Student's Role

Students design their approach to the lesson, including the following:

▶ Organize the different products of the lesson.

▶ Decide on the argument they want to present.

▶ Use the writing process to develop their script.

▶ Gather, organize, and edit footage or photos that support the written word.

▶ Select music and sound effects to use in their commercial that enhances the group's message.

▶ Publish the completed video to DVD.

With the teacher's guidance, the students should create a rubric to assess the outcomes of the project.

> **TIP** If you need help creating rubrics, Rubistar from www.4teachers.org is a free online rubric creator that supports multimedia projects.

Teacher's Role

Determine the criteria for evaluating student's work throughout the project and explain how you will assess the parts of the project, including:

▶ The ability of the group to capture, edit, and organize their persuasive argument.

▶ The use of the writing process for the creation of the group's script.

▶ The selection or acquisition of video footage or photos that support the group's position.

▶ The presentation of the commercial, focusing on clarity of message and overall persuasive and visual impact.

Establish and explain the criteria that will be used for evaluating the student's technical skills, including their ability to:

▶ Create and sort an organized list of persuasive arguments.

▶ Develop a script and storyboard that present the students' words and visuals in an organized manner.

▶ Capture high-quality visuals with attention being paid to visual composition and audio quality.

▶ Edit their material into a cohesive project using iMovie.

▶ Publish their work to a DVD using iDVD.

Be sure to explain to students how you will evaluate their ability to reach the goals and objectives of the project, as judged by the final product.

Getting Started

Teacher Planning

In order for the lesson to succeed, you will need a working knowledge of the technology, including:

▶ The basic functionality of Numbers, the spreadsheet application included with iWork (see Lesson 10 of *Apple Training Series: iWork '08*).

▶ The basic functionality of Pages, the word-processing application included with iWork (see Lesson 12 of *Apple Training Series: iWork '08*). A two-column video script template is included on the DVD-ROM of the iWork '08 book.

▶ The basic functionality of iMovie, the video editing application included with iLife (see Lesson 5 of *Apple Training Series: iLife '08*).

▶ The digital video or photo cameras available to students, so you can answer their questions. For an introduction to the basics of shooting video and loading it into your Mac, be sure to see Lesson 7 of *Apple Training Series: iLife '08*.

▶ It's a good idea to visit a video-sharing site, such as YouTube or SchoolTube, and choose a few examples of commercials or public service announcements that are similar in topic or focus to the student project.

▶ Develop guidelines for the length of the student commercials. Most television com-mercials run :30 or :60 seconds. The use of an exact run time makes the assignment more challenging and requires the students to choose and edit their words and visuals carefully and be mindful of communicating a succinct message.

▶ Develop guidelines for the content of the student presentations. This lesson plan is easy to modify for any age level or curricular area, so feel free to be creative. Many teachers find that putting the commercials into a historical perspective can be enjoyable for all involved. For example, a science class could use a public service announcement to raise awareness of significant historical discoveries such as gravity or DNA structure, while a history class could produce commercials debating amendments to the Constitution or take opposing sides in a past presidential race.

▶ Ensure that the needed hardware and software are available to the students.

▶ Determine the amount of time to be spent on the project, and provide suggested timeframes for project milestones. For example, how much time the students should spend shooting their footage or editing their commercial.

Student Preparation

It's a good idea to give the students some time to experiment with the hardware and software before they start creating their commercial or public service announcement. Ideally, let students:

▶ Explore Numbers and Pages.

▶ Practice editing video files. A useful practice exercise can be adapted from Lesson 5 of *Apple Training Series: iLife '08*.

▶ Students should explore the basics of creating a DVD with iDVD. A practice exercise can be adapted from Lesson 16 of *Apple Training Series: iLife '08*.

Introducing the Project

The first step in introducing the project is to show examples of effective commercials. The focus here should be less on commercial products and more on political or public service announcements. There are numerous examples online; here are a few to get you started:

▶ **All Politics – Ad Archive** – www.cnn.com/ALLPOLITICS/1996/candidates/ad.archive/

▶ **The :30 Second Candidate** – www.pbs.org/30secondcandidate/

▶ **Political Communication Lab** – pcl.stanford.edu/campaigns/

▶ **Internet Archive** – www.archive.org

▶ **Creativity** – www.creativity-online.com/

Next, present the students with a list of possible topics for their commercials. Consider placing student groups on opposite sides of an issue so they can evaluate the effectiveness of their commercial in comparison with that of the opposing side.

Earth Day Challenge

Jane Goodall Global Youth Summit

SOMETIMES THE POWER OF LEARNING reaches beyond the classroom and connects directly to social issues that touch all of our lives. In recent years, no scientific area has been of greater concern to young people than the environment. Learning about the threats of global warming and the deterioration of environments around the world makes young people want to take action.

Digital arts provide a way for students to express their concerns and ideas for the future, in some cases enabling them to take a leadership role for the first time. Educationally, students are learning the importance of applying media conventions to their arguments. Digital film is a powerful extension of their voice, but what exactly is their argument? How do they persuade their audience to embrace their solutions?

In response to such questions, the Digital Arts Alliance launched the Mobile Learning Institute Earth Day Challenge. Starting at Jane Goodall's Global Youth Summit in the spring of 2008 and extending through the end of the year, thousands of students across the United States and around the world created short films about environmental topics.

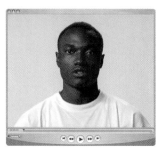

To kick off the Earth Day Challenge, the Digital Arts Alliance worked with 100 young people at the Global Youth Summit to make public service announcements on an array of environmental topics. Participants worked in teams, and each group involved students from diverse locations including Nepal, Spain, Kazakhstan, and China, as well as the United States.

The digital arts program allowed these young people to connect across their cultures using the environmental subjects that they cared about as a group. Some suggested topics at the summit were fresh water conservation, efficient energy use, air pollution, and rainforest conservation.

These short films demonstrate how young people can use digital arts to integrate what they know about science and society into powerful work— work that has been shared with all of the other students in the program and in local communities from Alabama to Dar es Salaam, Tanzania. You can learn more at www.earthdaychallenge.org.

The Jane Goodall Global Youth Summit and the Mobile Learning Institute are examples of ways that digital arts reach beyond the classroom. Digital film is a way that students can take action: by distributing their media pieces and, more broadly, by demonstrating to other young people that each of us can make a difference. To see examples of their work, visit www.digitalartsalliance.org/partnerships/goodall.

Creating the Project

There are several potential tasks to this project. You can adapt these to meet the educational goals and time constraints of your classroom, as well as the age and ability levels of your individual students.

Research the Issue

Once you divide them into groups, give the students time to research the topic they will be presenting. Students might want to divide their larger group into smaller topic groups for their research. The goal is to gather facts and opinions that can be used to make a case.

Depending upon your school's policy, consider giving students access to the Internet for researching a topic. Be sure to emphasize that students must build and refine their own script, not merely use an existing commercial or line of reasoning.

Develop & Organize Arguments

After adequate research time, have the students rejoin their group and encourage them to share their ideas on points to include in the argument. Be sure the group understands that the goal of this initial brainstorming is to capture all ideas and encourage participation in the discussion by all members of the group. The students can use Numbers to compile and organize a list of persuasive arguments.

1   Launch the Numbers application.

Depending on your computer's setup, you'll either find Numbers located in the Dock or by navigating to the iWork folder inside your Applications folder.

2   From the Template Chooser, select the Checklist template and click Choose.

A new, blank document opens. This is a checklist that can be adapted to help students develop and organize their arguments. It will need to be reformatted slightly for this stage of the writing process.

3   In the Sheets list, double-click the text labeling the sheet Checklist, and rename it *Arguments*.

4   Change the label of Column B to read *Ranking* and the label of Column C to read *Position*.

Column B is currently set up to format all entered data as a date; spreadsheets often format numbers to help clarify them. Changing formatting is easy.

5   Click the header of Column B so all the text is selected. In the Format Bar, click the button marked "1.0" to Format as a number with two decimal places.

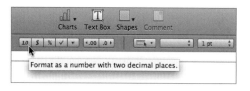

6   Click the ".0" button in the Format Bar two times, to decrease the number of decimal places. The formatting now should specify a whole number with no decimals.

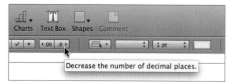

7   Have students enter their arguments into Column C. They should use one line per argument. Pressing the Return key will switch between cells.

8   Once the students have entered all of their positions, they'll need to sort their list so only the strongest points remain. This sorting process can be accomplished by debate within the group or by voting among group members.

9   For all positions that the majority of the group decides are valid, the students should place a check mark in column A.

Once the positions are initially selected, Numbers can hide the non-selected positions to make it easier to focus on just the points being made.

10   Click the Sort & Filter button in the toolbar. The Sort & Filter window opens.

The entries in the list can now be filtered to only show the selected items.

11   Select the checkbox next to "Show rows that match the following."

12   Select Column A from the first pop-up menu and set the filter value to true. Now only the selected items are shown.

13 Students can now discuss the relative strength of each position. The group should rank their positions numerically.

14 Students should enter the ranking for each position in column B, using 1 for the strongest argument and continuing to number sequentially.

15 To sort the positions from strongest to weakest, click column B so the entire column is selected.

16 In the Sort & Filter window, specify to sort Ranking ascending and click Refresh.

NOTE ▶ As a cross-curricular activity, students in each group can rank the positions individually. These ranks can be combined and averaged, and entered into Column B.

The students' positions are now in an organized list that can be used for the development of the script.

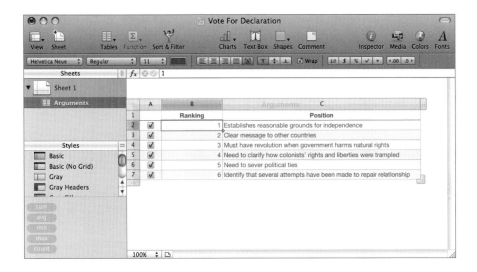

MORE INFO ▶ The spreadsheet features of Numbers are covered in Lesson 10 of the Apple Training Series iWork '08 book.

Write a Script

The next step in producing a commercial is to develop the script. Have the students use the points developed in the last exercise to create a compelling script that clearly makes a case with multiple supported points. Be sure to emphasize the need for creativity and storytelling rather than an on-camera lecture.

1   Launch Pages.

Depending on your computer's setup, you'll either find Pages located in the computer's Dock or by navigating to the iWork folder inside your Applications folder.

2   From the Template Chooser select the Word Processing group and then click the Miscellaneous category. Click the Screenplay template once and click Choose.

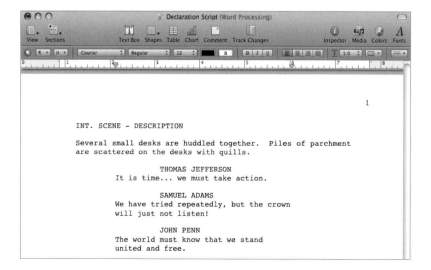

A new, preformatted document opens.

3   Students can type their script using standard word-processing functions.

4   Use standard formatting commands by accessing the Format Bar at the top of the document window.

5 Have students choose Edit > Spelling > Check Spelling when they want to examine their document for spelling and grammar errors.

6 Throughout the writing process, students should choose File > Save to capture their writing.

Students should store their work in a folder on the computer for the assignment.

As students progress through the stages of the writing process, they should review each point they are emphasizing. In the revising stage, they should critically examine each argument for clarity and focus.

7 To print a document, choose File > Print and select a printer on your classroom network.

NOTE ▶ Students should read their script aloud and act it out to test its effectiveness. This is also a good way to check the likely run time for the script.

MORE INFO ▶ The word-processing features of Pages are covered in Lesson 7 of *Apple Training Series: iWork '08*.

Create a Storyboard

Once the script is written, the group can refine their vision by converting the script into a storyboard. Storyboards are a visual tool that combines the words of the script with representative photos or drawings (they are similar to a comic book). The storyboard acts as a rough draft for all the visual elements of a production. For example, the pictures in the storyboard panel may represent each shot taken with a video camera that will make up the scene. The images also could represent still photos that will help convey the group's message. Pages offers an easy-to-use template for making a storyboard.

1 Launch Pages or choose File > New.

2 From the Template Chooser, select the Word Processing group and then click the Miscellaneous category. Click the Storyboard template once and click Choose.

A new, blank document opens using a storyboard layout.

3   Students can copy and paste lines of their script below each block. The goal is to break the script up so lines of text match with key visuals.

4   Once the text is filled in, choose Edit > Spelling > Check Spelling to check the document for spelling and grammar errors.

5   To print the document, choose File > Print and select a printer on your classroom network. Print 2 copies of the storyboard.

6   The students should then sketch in a visual for each scene of their commercial.

iStockphoto/urbancow

This is merely meant to help in planning video or still shots. Students can use stick figures or rough drawings as needed. The most important thing about a storyboard is that it will represent each image or video shot that will help tell a story or enhance the point the group is trying to make. It doesn't need to be a fine work of art; rather, it's a tool to communicate their planning. If the group can follow their storyboard, then they've accomplished their task. However, for more vibrant detail and clarity, it is suggested that students first draw in pencil, then return and outline in ink and fill in with markers or colored pencils.

Shoot Digital Video or Digital Photos

Students will need video footage or photos to complete their commercial. The approach taken here will vary based upon access to digital video or photo cameras and time allowed. Be sure to emphasize the following points for students shooting video:

▶ It's essential to let the camera roll 5 seconds before and after speaking. Sometimes known as "handles," this is called shooting pre- and post-roll and is important for editing purposes.

▶ Students should use a tripod (if available) so the video is stable and clear. If tripods are not available, brace the camera on flat surfaces such as desks or tabletops to minimize shaky video.

▶ Make students aware of basic lighting principles. In general, they should make sure their subject is well-lit, and should avoid shooting into a light source or the sun.

iStockphoto/Ju-Lee

▶   If there is a headphone jack on the camera, be sure students listen to the audio they are recording by plugging in a pair of headphones. This will give them a more accurate idea of background noise and the clarity of their audio.

▶   Instruct students not to over-record. Starting and stopping the camera between shots or takes is important and will save a lot of time during the editing stage. Each panel of the storyboard represents a separate shot for the video.

▶   Be sure students exercise caution while taping and that they respect the rules and property where they are staging their commercial.

Import Footage into iMovie

To edit their footage with iMovie, students will need to transfer the footage from the camera to their computer. This process of copying video from the camera onto a computer or hard drive is called "importing."

Remember, it can take many gigabytes (GB) of disk space to store video. For example Mini-DV cameras require 13 GB of storage for 1 hour of footage. Make sure the student's computers have enough storage space.

How you import footage will vary depending on whether your camera connects using a USB cable or a FireWire cable.

> **NOTE** ▶ If the students need to use photos in their commercial, simply import them into iPhoto. The pictures will be available in iMovie by clicking the Photos button (shaped like a digital photo camera).

Using a FireWire Connection

FireWire is the preferred connection type for loading video onto your computer if your camera uses tape. If your camera offers both USB and FireWire, choose to use FireWire. Make sure you have a 6-pin to 4-pin FireWire cable available.

1   Launch the iMovie application.

    You'll find iMovie located in the computer's Dock and inside your Applications folder.

2   Make sure the camera is turned off, then connect it to your computer using the FireWire cable.

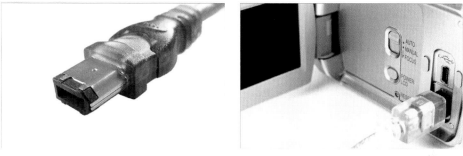

iStockphoto

    The 6-pin connector plugs into your Mac. The 4-pin connector plugs into your camera.

3   Turn the camera on and place it in VTR, VCR, or Play mode. The Import window opens.

    NOTE ▶ If the 1080i HD Import Setting dialog opens and you're not importing 1080i format video, just click OK.

4   In the Import window choose one of the two options from the lower-left side of the pane:

    ▶   **Automatic:** Rewinds the tape, imports the entire tape, and then rewinds the tape again. If using this option, click OK.

    ▶   **Manual:** Allows for manual rewind, fast-forward, and import of any part of the tape. If using this option, set the tape to the point that needs to be imported, then control playback using the playback controls. As the tape plays, click Import to begin importing.

5 Click Import.

6 Choose a disk to hold the imported video from the Save To pop-up menu.

7 Create a new Event to hold the students' video. Name the Event with the students' group name by typing it in the "Create new Event" field.

8 Click OK, and then do one of the following:

> ▶ If importing automatically, the computer will load the entire tape and will automatically rewind when the import is finished.

> ▶ If importing manually, click Stop when the desired section of video has been imported. Students can continue to start and stop importing as the tape plays through until all the desired video is imported.

Using a USB Connection

Some cameras, notably those that record to hard disk drives or DVDs (and not tapes), use a USB connection. This is also true if you are using a digital still camera that also records video. To import the video, you'll need to connect the device using a USB cable. Many cameras come with special USB cables for the end that connects to the camera.

1 Launch the iMovie application.

You'll find iMovie located in the computer's Dock and inside your Applications folder.

2 Make sure the camera is turned off, and then connect it to your computer using the USB cable.

3 Turn the camera on and place it in VTR, VCR, or Play mode.

NOTE ▶ Do not attempt to load miniDVDs from a video camera into your Mac. The discs are not designed to work with the computer and can damage your DVD drive.

4 The Import window opens automatically.

All of the clips on the camera will be displayed. Use the playback controls under the viewer to review the clips.

5   Choose one of the two options from the lower-left side of the pane:

   ▶ To import all clips, set the Automatic/Manual switch to Automatic, and then click Import All.

   ▶ To import some of the clips, set the Automatic/Manual switch to Manual. Deselect any clips you don't want and then click Import Checked.

6   Choose a disk to hold the imported video from the Save To pop-up menu.

7   Create a new Event to hold the students' video.

    Name the Event with the students' group name by typing it in the "Create new Event" field.

8   Click OK.

    NOTE ▶ It can take from several minutes to more than an hour for iMovie to import the video and generate thumbnail images of each clip. The wait is determined by the quantity of clips, the number of open applications, and the speed of the computer used. A circular progress indicator in the Import window shows you a time estimate.

Edit the Video with iMovie

Editing video with iMovie is an easy, but detailed, process. Many students find it intuitive and figure out the core features all on their own. To offer guidance on the editing process, here are some suggested resources that will help both teachers and student.

▶ **iLife Online Tutorials** – There are several web-based tutorials that show the key features of editing video. These can be accessed by choosing Help > Video Tutorials.

▶ *Apple Training Series: iLife '08* – The official Apple-certified guide offers six useful lessons on iMovie '08 covering both basic and advanced topics. Lesson 5, "Assembling a Simple Movie," is an excellent starting point for teachers and offers hands-on practice files that can be used in the classroom.

> **NOTE** ▶ Students will often want more time to create a well-edited finished product. Unfortunately the time constraints in the classroom might prevent this. The most essential element of the video creation process is to edit the footage and place it in a logical sequence that helps tell the story or communicate the point. Even if all the students do is this step, then they have a story with the essence of what they wanted to communicate.

> When students complete the editing and placement of footage, they can begin adding elements that will make their project more professional looking. Titles and credits should be added next so that students can introduce their topic and cite any sources they used for their project.

> Although some people feel that a musical soundtrack should be added at the very end, a video project often looks more refined when it is edited with music in mind. Finding appropriate music can truly help communicate the story and reinforce the emotions and points that are made.

Add Music and Sound Effects with GarageBand

Once the video edit is complete, students can move the video project into GarageBand. This will allow the students to add music and sound effects. GarageBand is very versatile, so students can choose to use pre-recorded jingles and sound effects, create their own music using musical loops (pre-recorded sections of musical instruments), or even record their own music from scratch.

1   Before closing your iMovie project, choose Share > Media Browser.

2   Specify the Large size and click Publish.

Depending on the size of the project and speed of the computer, this may take a few minutes.

3   Launch the GarageBand application.

You'll find GarageBand located in the computer's Dock and inside your Applications folder.

4   In the GarageBand welcome screen, click the Create New Music Project button.

5   Name the project with the student's group name and save in the default location.

6   Click Create.

You'll need to customize the screen to see some elements for controlling the movie.

7   Choose Control > Show Loop Browser.

The Loop Browser lets you access short musical elements called loops that can be used to create custom music. You can also access musical jingles and sound effects by clicking the podcasts sound view button.

TIP One way to work collaboratively in the classroom is to distribute some of the elements of a project. If there are multiple computers available, some students can work on finding or creating appropriate music and sound effects, while other students continue editing. However, if students work on multiple computers, they will need to export their finished musical piece and transfer it to the computer with the video. If there are any appropriate sound effects chosen, students can write down the names of the sounds so that they can be more easily found on the computer with the video.

8   Choose Control > Show Media Browser. Click the Movies button to access the iMovie project.

9   Choose Track > Show Movie Track.

10 Click the Movies button in the Media Browser, select the iMovie project, and drag it into the Movie Track.

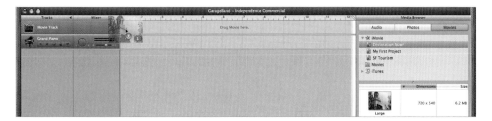

11 Students can now drag musical elements and sound effects into the tracks below. If an entire musical piece was created on another computer, they can either add the audio file into iTunes or drag it directly onto a GarageBand track after transferring to the computer with the video.

MORE INFO ▸ You can find more out about using GarageBand to create music by reading Lessons 11 & 13 of *Apple Training Series: iLife '08*. You can also choose Help > Video Tutorials to see short tutorials on the essential features of GarageBand.

12 When finished scoring the music, choose File > Close.

13 Click the Save button to capture changes.

14 When asked about saving your project with an iLife preview, click Yes.

This option generates a preview file that we can use in other iLife and iWork applications. We'll need it for use in iDVD.

Publishing the Project

Once the student group has completed their commercial, they'll need to prepare it for presentation to the class. By publishing the project to DVD, students can easily play their commercial on television sets with a DVD player or a computer with a DVD drive.

> **NOTE** ▶ Students will likely want to take their commercial home with them. You may want to have students burn extra copies of the DVD so they can each take one home. Creating a commercial is an accomplishment they'll want to share.

Publish as a DVD

Creating a DVD on a Mac is easy with iDVD. Your DVD can contain videos to watch or photo slideshows. For this project, students should add their finished commercials. If you have an advanced group, they can experiment adding other options like additional video tracks or slideshows.

1   Return to GarageBand and re-open the students' commercial project.

2   In GarageBand, choose Share > Send Movie to iDVD.

   iDVD launches and the video project is exported and sent to an iDVD project.

3   Quit GarageBand.

4   Students can change the text on any button by clicking once to select the button, then once again to highlight the text.

5   Click the Themes pop-up menu or pick a theme to change the look of the DVD menu.

   After picking a theme, click Change to apply it. Most menus have empty areas called drop zones.

6   Students can drag photos or video from the Media Browser into a drop zone to customize the menu.

7   When you are ready to test the DVD, click the round Play button at the bottom of the iDVD window.

The iDVD window turns into a preview window and brings up the iDVD remote control. Students should test all their buttons on the DVD and make sure the simulated DVD works.

NOTE ▶ If the project looks distorted, try choosing Project > Switch to Standard (4:3) or Switch to Widescreen (16:9).

8   When finished previewing, click the Exit button on the remote.

9   Choose Project > Project Info.

10   Give the DVD a name that identifies it with the students' group.

     You'll want to keep the name short. You can also change other information about the
     DVD here such as the Aspect Ratio (if you want the DVD to be widescreen) and set
     the Encoding method for quality.

11   Close the Project Info window.

12   Click the Burn button at the bottom of the iDVD window.

13 Insert a blank recordable DVD into the Mac's optical drive.

When iDVD finishes creating the first DVD, it ejects the disc and gives you the oppor-tunity to make additional copies. These copies are created much faster as the disc is already built. Students can make their own personal copies of the project.

NOTE ▶ If you need to move the iDVD project to another machine, choose File > Archive Project.

MORE INFO ▶ You can find more out about creating DVDs by reading Lesson 16 of *Apple Training Series: iLife '08* from Peachpit Press.

Assessing the Project

There are several ways to evaluate the student's performance for the lesson. Be sure to evaluate all aspects of the project, looking at the creativity and effectiveness of the commercial, as well as the technical performance of the tasks.

▶ Students should submit their scripts and storyboards in printed form and include any drafts and revisions for evaluation of the writing process. These can be assessed using standard practices or district guidelines for writing samples.

▶ Assess the students' performance of their commercial. Keep in mind the effectiveness of their story or commercial. Be sure to incorporate opportunities for peer review.

▶ Invite discussion, journal entries, or other follow-up activities regarding the project to assess the effectiveness of individual group members in creating the commercial.

▶ Have students complete self-assessment rubrics to justify their achievements in making a case.

4

Goals

Select a career and research the typical income and costs associated with it.

Create a budget template for family expenses.

Compare multiple spending scenarios, and analyze monthly expenses.

Select a vacation destination and estimate costs associated with the trip.

Create a poster to track progress towards saving money for the vacation.

Write a short summary report analyzing the affordability of the vacation.

Requirements

Recommended hardware and software:

▶ Macintosh computers

▶ Numbers (part of iWork '08)

▶ Pages (part of iWork '08)

▶ Internet access

▶ Color printer

Lesson 4

Solve a Problem: Reconcile a Household Budget

A relevant, real-world application for math is solving a budgeting problem. Students make a real-world decision, analyzing income and expenses, weighing their spending options, and ultimately deciding whether to make a large expenditure or not. Teaching students to use math and problem-solving skills within the context of a real life problem helps them understand the role of math in everyday life.

Using a spreadsheet helps students experiment with and compare different financial scenarios. Through an exercise like this, students are able to analyze financial data, arrive at a conclusion, and back up that decision with solid reasoning based on mathematical facts.

Project Summary

iStockphoto/chrisboy2004

As part of a lesson in math or career planning, students produce a budget to evaluate their household expenditures. Students choose which purchases to make in order to balance their budget. By using Numbers, students can quickly compare spending scenarios on a single spreadsheet.

In order to deepen student knowledge and augment the exercise, you can introduce several variables. Students can select a career and ascertain the average salary for that particular job. You can also introduce unexpected variables that affect the student's savings, such as home repairs, job bonuses, or an unexpected medical expense.

Once the initial budget is built, students pick a vacation destination and estimate the costs associated with their intended trip. They create a savings plan for the trip, and design a poster using Pages to track their savings progress. Finally, they defend their decision as to whether the trip is affordable or not.

Learning Objectives

After completing this project, students will be able to:

Academic

▶ Develop a logical approach for solving problems.

▶ Use critical thinking to make decisions between different options.

▶ Evaluate the fiscal impact of decisions about career and spending.

▶ Work in a partner setting, sharing responsibilities and learning to compromise to successfully complete the project.

▶ Analyze financial data, then create a summary report that clearly presents the group's decisions and rationale.

Technical

▶ Use the Internet to evaluate different cost options for products and services.

▶ Use a spreadsheet to model and evaluate the financial scenarios.

▶ Use Numbers to calculate individual costs of items.

▶ Use Pages to build a poster for tracking progress towards a goal.

Assessment Guidelines

iStockphoto/borisyankov

Student's Role

Students design their approach to the lesson, including the following:

- ▶ Organizing the products of the lesson (spreadsheet, poster).

- ▶ Researching careers and average salaries.

- ▶ Deciding on expenditures for their annual budget.

- ▶ Gathering and organizing their financial scenarios.

- ▶ Designing a progress-tracking poster.

- ▶ Creating a short summary report to accompany their data.

With the teacher's guidance, the students should create a rubric to assess the outcomes of the project.

Teacher's Role

Determine the criteria for evaluation of student's work throughout the project and explain how you will assess the parts of the project, including:

- ▶ The ability of the student pairs to work collaboratively and make effective compromises regarding household budget.

- ▶ The use of the writing process for the creation of the group's summary document.

- ▶ The use of spreadsheets to calculate costs associated with different scenarios.

- ▶ The use of modeling tools to display the financial options.

- ▶ The design of the group's poster.

Be sure to explain to students how you will evaluate their ability to reach the goals and objectives of the project, as judged by the final product.

Getting Started

Teacher Planning

In order for the lesson to succeed, the teacher will need a working knowledge of the technology and resources the students will use:

▶ The basic functionality of Numbers, the spreadsheet application included with iWork (see Lesson 10 of *Apple Training Series: iWork '08*).

▶ The basic functionality of Pages, the word-processing application included with iWork (see Lessons 7 and 8 of *Apple Training Series: iWork '08*).

▶ Identify websites ahead of time that show the different expenses associated with the lesson. These should include utilities, real estate, auto, etc. Where possible, use local expenses, as national averages may not be realistic for your area of the country.

▶ Identify resources students can use to investigate careers and related salaries. For jobs that require advanced training, be sure to have students calculate financial loan costs.

▶ Ensure that the necessary hardware and software are available to the students.

▶ Determine the amount of time to be spent on the project. Provide guidelines for project milestones. For example, how much time the students should spend deciding on their vacation destination.

Student Preparation

Tell the students the lesson objectives in advance, so they have time to prepare.

▶ Give students time to explore Numbers and Pages.

▶ Have students think about possible career options in advance.

Math at the Movies

TO REALLY UNDERSTAND MATHEMATICS, Students need to understand the concepts behind the facts. Nothing reflects deep knowledge more clearly than the ability to explain it to others. Digital arts projects allow students to explain, express, and explore. And well-articulated explanations can be used from class to class, to tutor other students. Allowing a student to hear an explanation from another student can be an effective strategy that gives classwork ongoing life.

The idea of constructing an explanation of what one knows is especially relevant in geometry, an area of math that often depends on memorization. Digital arts projects offer students a new approach in which they integrate what they know in the course of making the digital film.

At Teach Elementary in California's San Luis Coastal Unified School District, Miss Lamphier's students collaborated in groups to create digital films as part of a unit on geometry. The process required team members to work cooperatively in order to write clear and accurate narrations about a specific geometry topic. Throughout the activity, students not only applied math skills, technology, and life skills, but also expanded their creative and critical-thinking capacities.

Mathematics is also a broad subject with deep historical roots and one that is applied everywhere in the world around us. It is a subject full of stories of people, invention, and intellectual curiosity. Digital stories about mathematics let students dig into that rich context in a way that makes the subject come alive.

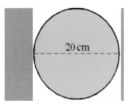

In Irving, Texas, at Austin Middle School, Ms. Williamson's second-period math students made digital stories about mathematicians, math theorems, and important moments in math history.

Mathematics is part of the world around us, especially in the realm of architecture. Fifth-graders at San Jose Elementary School in California made digital stories about their experiences studying with a professional architect, Todd Smith.

During the course of a residency during which Mr. Smith visited Mr. Gamarra's class once a week, the architect introduced the students to the basics of architecture and took them on a field trip with other fifth-graders to the Walt Disney Concert Hall, a remarkable building designed by world-famous architect Frank Gehry. He also advised the students as they broke into small groups and created their own architectural models. At the end of the project, the models were included in a display for viewing by fourth-grade classes. To see their work, visit www.digitalartsalliance.org/peachpit/teachersguide.

Introducing the Project

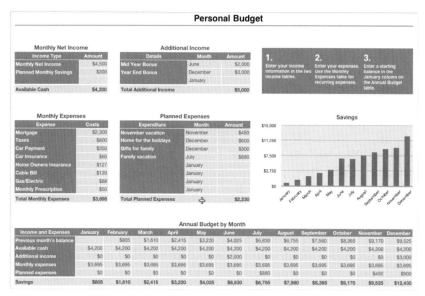

The first step is to discuss the role that budgets play in households. Open the existing budget template in Numbers and print out enough copies for your class. Lead a discussion as you evaluate the different categories on the budgeting worksheet. Be sure that students understand how different items work together in determining household budgets.

Next, pair the students into groups of two. These student groups will evaluate several criteria in balancing their budgets. Their first job will be to determine their fictitious career paths.

You can vary the complexity of the tasks in this project and adapt them to match your educational goals and time constraints. For example, the lesson can be streamlined for a math class, with the number variables simplified to expedite the project. On the other end, in a career development course, students can do more research into their career options and choose between multiple career paths.

Select a Career

iStockphoto/YinYang

There are several ways to implement this first task. It is up to you what constraints you place on the students' career selection process. Here are two scenarios you can use, depending upon your goals for the lesson.

Job Pool

Offer a pool of different jobs to select from. Working in pairs, students can randomly draw a career from the pool. You can choose to give students information about the salary of the jobs as well as provide information about the cost of education. This is a good approach if you want to streamline this first stage.

Job Search

Let the students, working in pairs, choose careers based upon their interests and goals. Be sure the students choose job categories that are broad enough to support salary research, and that they research the average salary associated with their desired jobs.

Create a Personal Budget Worksheet

After adequately researching their careers, students should create a personal budget worksheet to balance their household budget. Fortunately, Numbers offers an easy-to-use template that only needs a little bit of customization. The students can use Numbers to list and organize their expenses throughout the exercise.

1 Launch the Numbers application.

Depending on your computer's setup, you'll either find Numbers located in the computer's Dock or by navigating to the iWork folder inside your Applications folder.

2 From the Template Chooser, select the Budget template and click Choose.

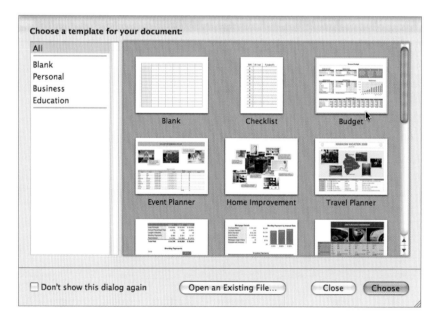

A new document opens. This is a budget that can be adapted to work for the students' exercise. It will need to be reformatted slightly.

3   In the Sheets list, double-click the text labeling the sheet Checklist and rename it with the students' names.

4   Repeat for the title on the page as well.

Susan Branch & John Davis Household Budget

5   Click the Monthly Net Income table to select it.

6   Enter the household income for monthly net income.

If a formula is needed, use something like this (Job A and Job B here represent the annual salary earned by each member of the group):

= (Job A + Job B)/12

	A	B		Additional Income		
	Income Type	**Amount**		**Details**	**Month**	**Amount**
1						
2	Monthly Net Income	=(42000+30000)/12		us	June	$2,000
3	Planned Monthly Savings	$300		Year End Bonus	December	$3,000
4					January	
5	Available Cash	$5,700		Total Additional Income		$5,000

7   Enter an amount into the planned monthly savings.

This amount should be between 5% and 15% of the Monthly Net Income cell.

8   Click the Additional Income table to select it.

9   Enter expected revenue (if any) not covered by the group's salary.

Monthly Net Income				Additional Income		
Income Type	Amount			Details	Month	Amount
Monthly Net Income	$6,000		2	Summer Job	July	$1,500
Planned Monthly Savings	$500		3	Year End Bonus	December	$3,000
			4	Coaching Camp	August	$400
Available Cash	$5,500		5	Total Additional Income		$4,900

This can include bonuses, financial investments, or part-time jobs. Let students know that they can revisit this additional revenue later in order to balance their budget, but must be able to justify the amount of money entered.

NOTE ▸ To erase a cell, simply highlight it and press the Delete key.

MORE INFO ▸ The spreadsheet features of Numbers are covered in Lesson 10 of *Apple Training Series: iWork '08.*

Calculate Monthly & Planned Expenses

Balancing a budget requires that the students make decisions about how to spend their money. Have the students generate a list of monthly expenses that they expect to incur.

They can use the list of expenses in the budget template as a starting point, but should also generate their own items and costs. Students should be prepared to cite their sources when assigning costs. The Internet is a useful tool for checking costs.

1   Delete all values in the Amount column for both Monthly and Planned Expenses tables.

2   Determine your monthly expenses.

Students should research the costs for things like mortgages, car insurance, and utility bills.

3   Click the Monthly Expenses table to select it.

4   Enter your expenses for the categories listed or modify the list.

If additional rows are needed, choose Table > Add Row Below.

5   Be sure to check that the Total Monthly Expenses formula calculates all costs.

Monthly Expenses			Planned Expenses		
Expense	Costs		Expenditure	Month	Amount
Mortgage	$2,500		Summer Vacation	July	
Taxes	$350		Home for the Holidays	December	$600
Car Payment	$450		Gifts for Family	December	$450
Car Insurance	$60		Home Improvements	September	$3,000
Home Owners Insurance	$165		Spring Break Trip	April	$900
Cable Bill	$80			January	
Gas/Electric	$135			January	
Car Gas Bill	$160			January	
Food	$800		Total Planned Expenses		$4,950
Entertainment	$300				
Clothing	$140				
Total Monthly Expenses	$5,140				

6   Click the Planned Expenses table to select it.

7   Students should enter all additional expenses they anticipate incurring, leaving the vacation trip field empty.

Determine Vacation Plans

Next, have the students determine how much money they have left over, and plan a vacation accordingly. You may want to have students create an additional spreadsheet to total the costs of their trip. Be sure students account for the following categories on their trip:

iStockphoto/skodonell

- ▶ Lodging
- ▶ Air Transportation
- ▶ Ground Transportation
- ▶ Meals
- ▶ Entertainment

1   Once a vacation amount is calculated, have students enter it into the Planned Expenses table.

2   Ensure that the budget is balanced and adequate funds are in savings.

3   Have students print out a copy of all budgets to submit for grading.

Prepare a Poster to Track Savings

Once the students have completed their budget, they can create a poster to track their progress in saving for the vacation. The poster should serve both as a reminder of the financial goals they are striving for and as a tool for tracking their progress towards their goal.

1   Launch Pages. The Template Chooser opens.

2   Click the Page Layout category and choose Posters, then select one of the templates, and click Choose.

A new, untitled document opens. The poster is ready to be designed. Students need to replace the placeholder text on the poster so that it contains the information needed. This is an easy process that involves just a little typing.

3   Double-click any text block and replace the placeholder text.

> **TIP**   If needed, you can disable hyphenation in the Text Inspector by clicking the More button and selecting the "Remove hyphenation for paragraph" checkbox.

4   Click outside the text block to exit it.

TIP You can add additional text boxes by choosing Insert > Text Box.

5   Gather or take any photos you want to use in the poster, and import them into iPhoto. Students are encouraged to organize their images in iPhoto by gathering them all in an Event or Album.

6   In the toolbar, click the Media button to open the Media Browser; then choose Photos and click the iPhoto icon.

The contents of your iPhoto library will be displayed in the browser (if needed, click the disclosure triangle to reveal the contents of your iPhoto library).

7   Drag any photo from the Media Browser and drop it on any image placeholder.

The photo is added to your poster. If you need to resize an image, it's easy to do.

8   Click the Edit Mask button, then drag the corners of the photo to resize it.

When finished, click the Edit Mask button again.

TIP You can modify a photo by choosing View > Show Adjust Image.

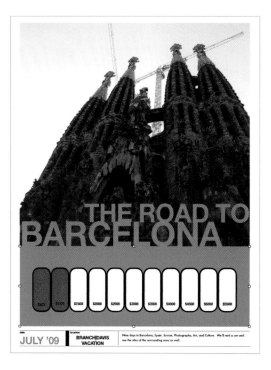

9   Have students create a progress bar using the drawing tools of pages.

Inserting a series of connected boxes is an easy way to track progress. Use one box for each $500 needing to be raised towards the trip's budget.

10   Save your work by choosing File > Save.

Publishing the Project

Once the student groups have completed their budgets, have them print all of the associated pieces for grading. Printing in Pages and Numbers is identical; students simply choose File > Print. Be sure to have students check their formulas before submitting.

The final item that students should include in their package for grading is a short summary document. Have the group discuss and defend their decision regarding expenses, income, and their planned trip. Depending on the age and ability level of the students, the summary will vary in length. The teacher should set clear guidelines on the expected length of the summary. For middle school and high school students, a two-page summary could be expected. Additionally, have students provide a list of sources used to determine values of expenses and revenues.

Assessing the Project

There are several ways to evaluate the student's performance for the lesson. Be sure to evaluate all aspects of the project, looking at the ability to solve a problem, as well as the technical presentation of the information.

▶   Students should submit their budgets and posters in printed form. These can be graded for accuracy and clarity in presentation.

▶   Assess the students' overall performance as a group.

▶   Invite discussion, journal entries, or other follow-up activities regarding the project to assess the effectiveness of individual group members in creating the commercial.

▶   Have students complete self-assessment rubrics to justify their achievements in making a case.

5

Goals

Develop a biographical story to tell and publish.

Identify a source to interview for the story.

Develop interview questions, record an audio interview, and gather optional supporting photos.

Record appropriate introductions and commentary to create a cohesive story/biography with the interview material.

Edit the acquired audio to create a three-to-seven-minute audio podcast.

Publish the podcast for distribution on portable media players and computers.

Requirements

Recommended hardware and software:

► Macintosh computers

► Digital audio recording devices with microphones

► Pages (part of iWork '08)

► GarageBand, iPhoto, and iWeb (part of iLife '08)

► Media hosting space (such as a web server) to host the podcast files and make them available to others

Tell a Story – Biography Podcast

Digital media is often used to help students understand information. Equally important, however, is teaching students to use digital tools to tell stories of their own. It is critical that students learn to make observations, gather information, edit the information, and organize it into a compelling story.

Podcasting is quickly emerging as an effective way to communicate with a potentially large audience. The term *podcasting* is used to describe the process of creating <u>P</u>ortable <u>O</u>n <u>D</u>emand media files for publication. Most often, a podcast is defined as a digital audio or video recording in the style of a radio or television news report. These reports are made available on the Internet, usually via subscription through an RSS feed, and can be downloaded to a personal media player or computer.

This new genre has dramatically increased citizen-based journalism. Podcasting has become popular because it allows people to tell stories in a compelling way and share them globally at low cost.

Project Summary

In this lesson, students pick an individual to be profiled in an audio podcast. Students produce a three-to-seven minute news report that features their narration as well as quotes from their interview subject. Each report should limit its focus to a single interview source and take a biographical approach to their subject. This lesson can be used in several different curricular areas and is easily adaptable. For example:

▶   A career development class can focus on creating profiles of different career options available to students.

▶   A class studying civics can offer students a chance to explore the running of a local government by interviewing politicians, city employees, and politically active members of the community.

▶   A health class could focus on issues facing young adults and produce compelling audio interviews.

▶   An art class could profile different local artists and the styles of their work. An audio podcast can also be enhanced with images, so it would be possible to hear from the artist and see their work.

There are excellent examples of podcasts on iTunes. A great place to start is by watching the overview of iTunes U at www.apple.com/education/itunesu_mobilelearning.

Students use Pages to create a list of questions for the interviewee. The students then interview their subjects, recording the interview and their own narration. This can be accomplished using portable audio recorders or laptop computers. Students then edit their podcasts together using GarageBand, enhance the program with photos, and publish it to share with others using iWeb.

Learning Objectives

After completing this project, students will be able to:

Academic

▶   Develop a theme for telling a story.

▶   Use interview skills to collect information.

▶   Use the writing process to create a script that tells the story and links the audio interview clips.

▶ Develop visual literacy by gathering images that support the spoken word.

▶ Edit and arrange interview and script into a compelling story.

Technical

▶ Use Pages to build a list of interview questions.

▶ Record an audio interview using a portable recorder or laptop.

▶ Record additional audio from a script to help tell the story.

▶ Shoot or acquire digital photos to enhance podcast (optional).

▶ Edit their audio clips and script together using GarageBand.

▶ Publish to the Internet with iWeb.

Assessment Guidelines

Student's Role

Students design their approach to the lesson, including the following:

▶ Decide on the person they want to profile and the story they want to tell.

▶ Use the writing process to develop interview questions and script.

▶ Gather, organize, and edit audio and photos that tell their story.

▶ Publish the completed audio podcast.

With the teacher's guidance, the students should create a rubric to assess the outcomes of the project.

Teacher's Role

Determine the criteria for evaluation of student's work throughout the project and explain how you will assess the parts of the project, including:

▶ The ability of the student to develop an interesting story that engages the audience.

▶ The use of the writing process for the creation of the script.

▶ The student's ability to interview their subject and explore their topic.

▶ The presentation of the podcast, focusing on ability to tell a story and overall impact.

Establish the criteria that will be used for evaluating the student's technical skills:

▶ The ability to create an organized list of questions for their subject.

▶ The capacity to record clear audio of the interview subject.

▶ Skill in editing audio and photo material into a cohesive project using GarageBand.

▶ Proficiency in publishing a story as a podcast using iWeb.

Be sure to explain to students how you will evaluate their ability to reach the goals and objectives of the project, as judged by the final product.

Getting Started

Teacher Planning

In order for the lesson to succeed, you'll need a working knowledge of the hardware and software used in this lesson, including:

▶ Watch a useful three-part video series about podcasting in the classroom, which can be found at www.apple.com/education/resources/podcastingvideos/.

▶ Understand the basic functionality of Pages, the word-processing application included with iWork (see Lesson 7 of *Apple Training Series: iWork '08*).

▶ Understand the basic functionality of iPhoto, specifically the ability to load digital photos into a computer (see Lesson 1 of *Apple Training Series: iLife '08*).

▶ Be familiar with the digital audio recording options available at your school. There are several ways to record audio, including iPods with recording adapters, dedicated digital audio recorders, laptops with microphones, or even audio chat with iChat. Be sure to discuss options with your technology support staff.

▶ Edit and post a sample podcast. Hands-on practice is the best way to learn the material (see Lessons 12 and 15 of *Apple Training Series: iLife '08*).

▶ Develop guidelines for the length of the student podcasts. Most audio podcasts run three to seven minutes.

▶ Develop guidelines for the content of the student podcasts. This will vary depending upon the class that this exercise is used for. This lesson plan can easily be modified for any curricular area or age level, so feel free to be creative.

▶ Ensure that the required hardware and software are available to the students. Be sure to determine how the podcast files will be hosted (and if they will be accessible outside of the school's computer network).

▶ Determine the amount of time to be spent on the project and provide time guidelines for achieving project milestones.

Student Preparation

The students should have some time to experiment with the hardware and software before creating their podcast.

▶ Give students time to explore Pages, GarageBand, and iWeb.

▶ Have students practice editing audio files. A useful practice exercise can be adapted from Lesson 12 of *Apple Training Series: iLife '08*.

▶ Students should explore the basics of creating a podcasting page using iWeb. A useful practice exercise can be adapted from Lesson 15 of *Apple Training Series: iLife '08*.

Introducing the Project

Successfully introducing the project is important to ensure student success. Start off by showing some examples of good student-produced podcasts. Fortunately, there are numerous excellent examples available. Try these:

▶ **An introduction to podcasting with GarageBand**–www.apple.com/ilife/tutorials/ #garageband-podcast-51

▶ **Apple Learning Interchange**–edcommunity.apple.com/ali/ collection.php?collectionID=466

▶ **Sample Podcasts on Apple Digital Authoring page**–www.apple.com/education/ digitalauthoring/podcasting.html

▶ **iTunes U**–deimos3.apple.com/indigo/main/main.xml

Students should also watch some podcasts or TV interviews that develop a story around interview questions. National Public Radio offers several excellent audio interviews in their podcasts, which may serve as a good model.

Tell me a Story

Informing Art, Creative Writing, and Social Science

WRITING IS THE SPINE OF A DIGITAL ARTS project. Well considered, written, and delivered narratives are the core of good digital films. Everything else in the project flows from the writing: the research, the storyboard, the final digital film.

Teaching in this way borrows more from conventional classroom practice than many teachers realize. If you know how to teach a subject area and writing and research, then you're well down the road to creating a digital arts project in your class.

The payoff for classroom activities such as those of the Digital Arts Alliance is that students can turn writing into a social activity, working in teams to go beyond simple exercises into ones that include argument and synthesis of multiple subjects and media. The projects provide a framework for students to connect to their subjects in new ways.

Let Me Tell You Who I Am...

Digital arts projects can help students to explore their own identity and the way that culture describes them. One way to guide this exploration in the classroom is to use a guiding question. This is exactly what teachers in San Diego did. Ms. Kania, Mr. Oster, and Mr. Hoskisson introduced eleventh-grade students to a final project by presenting the following question: *What influence have particular groups of people had on American culture?*

Students chose a sub-group in American society and focused on that guiding question, considering a range of people and populations including women of particular ethnic groups, gays, Muslim Americans, the disabled population, the working poor, Jewish Americans, Mormons, the KKK, white supremacists, hippies, Beat poets, Chicanos, zoot suiters, neo-conservatives, American socialists, American communists, war veterans, and others.

...And Who We Are...

In Oregon, at Madison High School, Mr. Grobey's leadership class used digital storytelling as the culminating project in their semester-long inventory and exploration of the strengths and weaknesses of their school community. Working in groups, students created documentaries to illustrate the three fundamental tenets of their school – demonstration, performance, and advocacy. Their goal involved demystifying or promoting their school, whether by identifying a weakness and advocating for improvement or by emphasizing existing strengths.

...And Who Katrina Was

The classroom is a place where students learn to make sense of their world. And in instances of great social stress, the opportunity to do so can be vital to helping young people understand and express their feelings about significant changes and dramatic events in the world around them.

Members of the Digital Arts Alliance witnessed this firsthand when we worked closely with students who had experienced the ravages of Hurricane Katrina. In cases such as this, a digital arts project is an opportunity to tie experience to opinion in a way that is cathartic for the young person creating the film. To see examples of their work, visit www.digitalartsalliance.org/peachpit/teachersguide.

Next, present the students with a list of possible people to profile and topics for their podcasts, and explain the interview process they will use. Depending upon your school's available technology, you may need to adapt the students' approach to interviewing in the field.

Planning the Project

The first step is to have students to select their story topic and identify an interview source. For some students, this will come easily. Others may need some guidance. Possible themes include a news-type story about a local issue or event and the role that the profiled person is playing or played; a biographical sketch of a local leader, artist, musician, or inspirational community member; or a retelling of an event in the student's own life, in which the profiled individual played a significant role.

Be sure to capture each student's idea, grant approval, and track ideas to avoid repetition or overlap. Student- or teacher-created checklists of activities can help guide students so that there is a systematic process for ensuring students have accomplished each step before moving on. If you don't want any topics repeated, then a Numbers spreadsheet or poster grid showing each student and their topic will help keep track of all the selections that have been made.

Because the interview process may involve students going into the "field" to capture their interviews, be sure to determine possible solutions for audio recording. Fortunately, the Macs in your classroom can accept a wide range of audio devices through their audio input jacks. Inexpensive studio-quality USB microphones are becoming a popular choice in classrooms due to their decent recording quality and low price.

Be sure to emphasize that students will be required to plan their interview questions in advance. By thinking through what they want to capture, they will have an easier time assembling their story. Perhaps the biggest mistake they'll make is capturing too much audio, leading to an overwhelming project. Be sure to emphasize keeping the topic and interview focused.

Creating the Project

There are several potential tasks to this project. You can adapt these as needed to meet the educational goals and time constraints of your classroom as well as the age and ability levels of your individual students.

Develop the Story

Give the students a defined time period to develop their stories. The teacher should be available to mentor the students during this period. The time allotted could be as simple as one night with a chance to discuss ideas with the teacher in class the next day. Be sure to challenge the students and help them refine their story's focus.

Once the student has identified an interview subject, they may need guidance on how to ask permission for the interview. This is an opportunity for role-play in the class to model proper approaches.

Develop Interview Questions

After adequate research time, have students develop a list of questions for their subjects. Encourage them to develop questions that will elicit detailed responses. To practice critical thinking skills and create a more in-depth interview, they should avoid questions that can be answered with a simple "yes" or "no." Tell students that some sources may prefer to see their questions in advance of the interview.

Developing the questions in advance also helps to organize the conversation and ensure that needed quotes are gathered to craft into the final story. Be sure a clear theme is present throughout the questions, and avoid going too broad in scope.

TIP ▶ One helpful exercise in creating effective interview questions is to have student volunteers role-play poor interview scenarios,such as an interview primarily made up of yes or no questions. They can also jump from topic to topic to demonstrate the need for a consistent theme.

1   Launch the Pages application.

Depending on your computer's setup, you'll either find Pages located in the computer's Dock or by navigating to the iWork folder inside your Applications folder.

2   From the Template Chooser, select the Blank template and click Choose. A new, blank document opens.

3   Type your interview questions using standard word-processing functions.

4   Use standard formatting commands by accessing the Format Bar at the top of the document window.

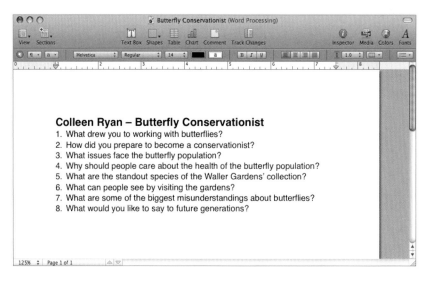

5   Choose Edit > Spelling > Check Spelling to examine the document for spelling and grammatical errors.

6   Throughout the writing process, choose File > Save to capture your work.

Students should store their work in a folder on the computer for the assignment.

7   To print a document, choose File > Print and select a printer on your classroom network.

MORE INFO ▶ The word-processing features of Pages are covered in Lesson 7 of *Apple Training Series: iWork '08.*

It's a good idea to have students turn their interview questions in for feedback or grading in advance of the interviews. You can then offer insights or suggestions to help the student improve their interviews. Encourage students to practice asking their questions. One common mistake is to create a well-written question that's hard to actually ask out loud.

Acquiring an Audio Interview and Photos

Have the students interview the subject of their story. The exact approach here will depend upon your school's policy for checking out audio recording devices. Be sure to adjust the lesson plan to account for limitations on audio recording equipment.

If equipment is limited and interviews are being conducted during school hours, be sure that interviewees are scheduled at different time slots to maximize your resources. You can use a Numbers spreadsheet to create a schedule of interviewees so that the students and teacher are able to keep track of all interviews and equipment. If students will be recording interviews off school property, be sure to discuss proper safety procedures (such as meeting in a public place or bringing a parent or other student with them).

Be sure to emphasize the following points for students recording audio.

▶   Let the audio device roll 5 seconds before and after speaking. This is called capturing pre- and post-roll, and is important for editing purposes.

▶   Make sure to keep the microphone about 8-12 inches away from the person who is speaking.

▶   Listen to the audio as it is recorded by plugging a pair of headphones into the recording device.

▶   Be careful not to over-record. Keeping the interview a reasonable length (no more than four times longer than the delivery time) will ensure that the editing stage does not become onerous.

▶ Exercise caution while recording for their personal safety.

▶ Show proper respect for their interview subjects by showing up on time, conducting the interview professionally, and sticking to their allotted time slot.

iStockphoto/kreci

Additionally, students may choose to enhance their podcasts using photos. These can be pictures they take of their interview subject or ones they borrow or purchase online. Be sure to emphasize that students show great care when working with other people's photographs.

> **TIP** ▶ If students are recording with the built-in microphone, they can also utilize Photo Booth and the iSight camera to take a photo of their interview subject.

Recording audio for a podcast in GarageBand can be as easy or complicated as needed for your project. For example, if your podcast needs only one voice track (which can contain more than one speaker), you can record the narration by connecting a microphone to your computer or by using the built-in microphone (if it has one). This could be the built-in iSight camera, which works because it includes a fully functioning microphone. Additionally, you can record remote interviews directly to GarageBand with iChat users.

Before recording, make sure that your equipment is turned on and properly connected to the computer. For more specifics on the operation of your equipment, refer to the equipment manuals.

Creating a New Podcast Project

Setting up a new podcast project is easy. GarageBand offers a useful New Podcast Episode template right in the GarageBand welcome screen. If students are able to take laptops to their recording sessions, they can record directly into GarageBand.

1   Launch GarageBand by clicking its icon in the Dock.

2   In the GarageBand welcome screen, click the New Podcast Episode button.

3   Have the students name and save their project to the GarageBand projects folder (the default location).

4   Click Create.

The Podcast Template project opens, with the empty Podcast Track, editor with marker information, and Media Browser already showing.

The Media Browser contains buttons for three different types of media files (Audio, Photos, Movies), a browser where you can navigate to the media files you want to use, and a media list showing the media files in the current location.

5   In the Timeline, male students should double-click the Male Voice track header; female students should double-click the Female Voice track. (Although using the wrong track won't dramatically change a voice, there are presets that will help enhance a voice when the correctly designated track is used.)

The Track Info pane appears for the selected track. Notice that the Podcasting instrument category has been selected, and Male Radio is the specific preset.

There are five Male Voice presets: iSight Microphone Male, Male Narrator Noisy, Male Narrator, Male Radio Noisy, and Male Radio.

The presets with *Noisy* in the title include an automatic noise-reduction filter to help eliminate unwanted background noise in the track.

The iChat and iSight presets are made for tracks using those types of recordings.

6 Select the Narrator preset that best matches the recording environment.

If the students have a microphone attached to their computer via the Audio input or USB port, they can record their interview. Be sure that the track you want to record on is selected and the Record Enable button is turned on (it's the little button by the track icon).

To begin recording, click the big red Record button or type the shortcut R. The easiest way to pause playback or recording is by pressing the spacebar.

> **NOTE ▶** If students used a recording device other than the computer, the audio files will need to be transferred to the computer. Digital audio recorders can usually transfer files via a USB cable. Analog audio devices can be connected and recorded (just like a microphone) in real-time. If students are using an iPod with a third-party microphone, the audio file will transfer to iTunes automatically the next time the iPod is synchronized. It will appear in the Voice Memo playlist. If it's recorded in high quality (a setting on the iPod), it can be dragged into the project via the Media Browser in GarageBand.

Editing the Podcast

Once the interviews are recorded, students select the sound bites they want to use. Students should listen to their interviews and take notes of which parts they want to use. Some students may find that an easy solution is to split the longer interview up into smaller pieces.

1 Move the playhead to the start of an interview question.

2 Choose Edit > Split to split the track at the playhead.

3 Move the playhead to the start of the next question and choose Edit > Split.

4 Repeat for each question until all the interview questions have been segmented.

TIP ▶ If students record a few seconds of silence before asking each question, they should be able to visually identify where to segment the audio. The lack of waveform indicates silence.

5 Review the interview question list and responses.

The goal here is for the students to order their interview responses and edit any information from the interview they don't want to include. For some students, editing audio will be intuitive, other students can roughly transcribe their interviews to note cards and try to determine the order of their sound bites. Students will need to record additional narration to help link the interview segments and develop a cohesive story (much like a news reporter).

NOTE ▶ There are several excellent tutorials on editing audio that are viewable by choosing Help > Video Tutorials. You can also see Lesson 12 of the *Apple Training Series: iLife '08.*

Working with Artwork

The next step is to enhance the audio with artwork or photos. In this way, the student can add a layer of visual understanding that reinforces the audio interview and demonstrates their knowledge of visual literacy.

When you add episode artwork to a podcast, the artwork appears when you play the podcast episode in iTunes (or on an iPod) and when you work with it in iWeb.

Artwork added to the Podcast Track creates a marker region the same length as the artwork in the Podcast Track. Marker regions are used in podcasts to literally *mark* a specific region in the Timeline to include artwork, a chapter title, or a URL. When you publish your podcast as an AAC file, iWeb or other software will use these marker regions to include the designated information for that region in the project.

The easiest way to access photos is to create an Event or Album in iPhoto. Have students import their images into iPhoto. If all the images are imported at the same time, a new Event will be created with those photos. If students are importing their photos at different times, it may be easier to create an Album that contains all the images they will need for their project, because each import will be a new Event. Students can make any adjustments needed to their images using iPhoto's editing tools.

> **MORE INFO** ▶ The iPhoto Help menu includes several excellent tutorials on working with photos. Choose Help > Video Tutorials. You can also see Lessons 1-4 of *Apple Training Series: iLife '08.*

Once the photos are ready, switch back to GarageBand by clicking the GarageBand icon in the Dock.

1   If the Media Browser is not visible, click the Media Browser button in the lower-right corner to open the Media Browser.

2   In the Media Browser, click the Photos button to show the Photos pane.

3 Click the Events button or Album where the images have been organized.

4 Double-click a specific Event or Album to see only those photos.

5 Click in the Timeline and press Return to move the playhead to the beginning of the project.

6 Select the Podcast Track to see it in the Track Info pane. The Track Info pane acts as a viewer for the images when the audio has been enhanced.

7 If not visible, press Command-E to show the editor. (Alternatively, you can click the Track Editor button, indicated by the icon of a pair of scissors, to activate the editor.)

The editor appears for whichever track is currently active. In this case, it will be the Podcast Track. The Episode Artwork well on the side of the editor is empty until an image is placed it it.

The Podcast Preview pane shows that no artwork is available, because the playhead is at the beginning of the project where there is no artwork in the Podcast Track.

8 Pick a photo to represent the entire podcast and drag it into the Episode Artwork well.

NOTE ▶ The Episode Artwork is often used for the logo of a Podcast series or organization. Schools often use their own logo or a modified one to showcase the podcast channel. For the purposes of this lesson, students can use an image of the interviewee or a school or class logo.

9 Select the image you want to display when the Podcast begins playing and drag it from the Media Browser to the beginning of the Podcast Track in the Timeline and release the mouse button.

The first image will span the whole podcast from the beginning to end. There is no need to shorten the image length, because each additional image will truncate the previous one and replace it from the point where it is dragged in.

10 Listen to the podcast as you place the appropriate images on the Podcast Track. Press the spacebar to play the podcast. When you hear the section where the next photo should be displayed, press the spacebar again to pause playback.

TIP ▶ Students can use a Storyboard to plan which image will go with each question. This helps speed up the editing process because students are more prepared for adding the visual elements to enhance their podcast.

11 From the Media Browser, drag the next photo into the Podcast Track.

12 Repeat for the remaining images.

TIP As students add images, they may notice that some of the images do not display the way they want them to. Sometimes the images may not be centered correctly or may show too much background. To adjust the cropping or centering of a photo, double-click it in the Artwork column to open the Artwork Editor. Adjust zoom and position, and click the Set button to save the settings for that image.

TIP You may want to break longer interviews up into chapters. Simply enter a chapter name into the Chapter Title field, located next to the Artwork list near the bottom of the window. Chapters allow listeners to navigate a long podcast more easily, as a listener can jump ahead or go back to a particular section.

Adding Episode Info to a Podcast

The last step is to add the episode information, which includes the title, artist information, a description of the episode, and a parental advisory. The episode information is available when you work on the podcast in iWeb and when you view the podcast in iTunes.

1 Select the Podcast Track in the Timeline.

2   Show the Track Info pane, if it is not already showing.

3   Click the Description area and enter descriptive information about the podcast and its creator.

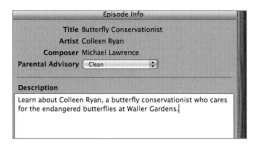

4   Press Command-S to save the finished podcast.

5   Play the podcast from start to finish to see the completed project.

Congratulations! You have successfully created a podcast! You can now publish it using iWeb.

NOTE ▶ As students watch and listen to the podcast, encourage them to observe the Track Info pane carefully. If there are any gaps in images, the Episode Artwork will display. If there is no Episode Artwork, they will have gaps where the message, "No Artwork Available" will show.

Publishing the Project

Once the podcast is done, it can be published with iWeb. In order to make the files available on the Internet, you will need to have access to web-hosting space, which is sometimes available through your school's Internet provider. If hosting is not an option, students can still complete the iWeb publishing for local viewing. Podcast files can also be distributed on removable media such as hard drives, CD-ROMs, or iPods.

NOTE ▶ Discuss your school's web publishing policy with the appropriate technology staff before publishing.

Publish as a Podcast

Publishing a podcast with iWeb is straightforward. Even students who know little about web page creation will be able to easily share their work.

1 In GarageBand choose Share > Send Podcast to iWeb.

A window drops down asking for settings to be specified. The default presets work well.

2 Click Share.

GarageBand prepares the podcast episode for delivery. This process can take a few minutes as the file is encoded and the artwork track embedded. When GarageBand finishes, it sends the episode to iWeb and creates a new blog or podcast entry in a website.

3 GarageBand may prompt you, asking for permission to use the keychain. Click Allow.

4 iWeb opens and a prompt appears asking you to pick a template and a page style. Choose an appropriate template and Podcast page style that will help enhance the story.

5   You can customize the web page in iWeb by using its many page-customization tools.

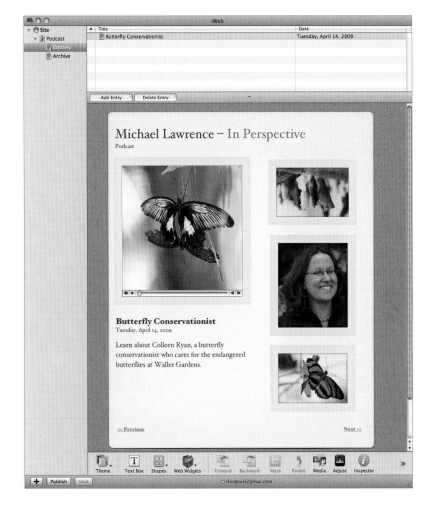

MORE INFO ▶ The iWeb Help menu includes several useful tutorials on customizing web pages. Choose Help > Video Tutorials. You can also see Lessons 14 and 15 of *Apple Training Series: iLife '08*.

6   Open the Blog & Podcast Inspector by clicking the Inspector button in the toolbar.

7   Choose the Podcast section and enter information about the podcast.

8   Have the students enter the teacher's contact email address in case there are any issues with the podcast.

9   Deselect the checkbox for Allow Podcast in iTunes Store.

10   Publish the site using your school's dictate procedure. This may be accomplished by choosing File > Publish to MobileMe or File > Publish to Folder and using a File Transfer Protocol application.

11   Have the students close iWeb and GarageBand and be sure to save their work.

   NOTE ▶ It is likely that the District will allow you, as a teacher, to publish a web page even if students are not allowed to do so. If this is the case, then have students Share their podcast to iTunes or to Disk (their computer's hard drive). The finished .m4a file can be transferred to your main computer, and all the projects can be published on your iWeb page.

Assessing the Project

There are several ways to evaluate the student's performance for the lesson. Be sure to evaluate all aspects of the project, looking at how well the story engages its audience as well as the technical skills used to capture and publish the podcast.

▶ Students should submit their interview questions and scripts in printed form and include any drafts and revisions for evaluation of the writing process. These can be assessed using standard practices or District guidelines for writing samples.

▶ Assess the students' performance in creating their podcast. Keep in mind the effectiveness and consistency of the questions that were asked. Be sure to incorporate opportunities for peer review.

▶ Invite discussion, journal entries, or other follow-up activities regarding the project to assess individual efforts.

▶ Have students complete self-assessment rubrics to justify their achievements in telling a story.

The 5 Tips that Classroom Teachers Use Most

Not only can iLife and iWork open up new possibilities in the classroom, but they can also make everyday classroom tasks easier. Our goal here is to help you create effective classroom materials without a lot of work on your part.

To jumpstart your efficiency, we offer tips for the 5 most-common tasks that teachers perform every day in the classroom—things like creating a quiz or a poster, or making a checklist. Many more tips are available free online on the book's companion web page at www.peachpit.com/ats.teachersguide, including how to add a short movie to a slideshow presentation or a web page, how to correct exposure in images or movies, and how to convert a presentation to DVD.

Tip #1: Make a Poster

Posters are a cost-effective way to promote an event or idea. They offer a large canvas for communicating ideas with text and visuals. Posters are best used to promote just a single concept, as they are often only quickly glanced at in passing. They can be used in any curricular area and help students learn how lay out information succinctly and effectively.

Pages (part of iWork '08) offers eight poster styles. Each one comes in two sizes: Large and Small. The exact dimensions of the poster will vary based on your country, but will match the standard paper sizes your printer uses. In the United States, for example, Large posters are 11 x 17 inches, and Small posters are 8.5 x 11 inches (an acceptable size for a flyer). Let's create a large-sized poster.

1   Launch Pages.

The Template Chooser opens.

2   Click the Page Layout category and choose Posters, then select one of the templates and click Choose.

A new, untitled document opens.

3   Choose File > Save; name the file and store it on your local hard drive.

The poster is ready to be customized for your classroom needs. The first step is to replace the placeholder text on the poster so that it contains the essential information. This is an easy process that involves just a little typing.

4   Double-click any text block. Replace the placeholder text simply by typing your new text.

You can easily modify text properties or shape properties by using the Format Bar at the top of the window.

TIP Most professionally created posters do not break up longer words with hyphenation because it isn't as visually appealing. You can disable hyphenation in the Text Inspector by clicking the More button and checking the "Remove hyphenation for paragraph" box. This forces a hyphenated word to close up on a single line where it can fit.

5   Click outside the text block to exit it.

TIP You can add additional text boxes by choosing Insert > Text Box.

6   In the toolbar, click the Media button to open the Media Browser.

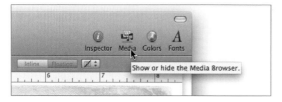

7   Choose Photos and click the iPhoto icon.

The contents of your iPhoto library will be displayed in the browser (if needed, click the triangle to reveal the contents of your iPhoto library).

8   Drag any photo from the Media Browser and drop it on any image placeholder.

The photo is added to your poster and will automatically fit into the placeholder. If you need to resize an image, it's easy to do.

9 Click the Edit Mask button, then drag the corners of the photo to resize it. When finished, click the Edit Mask button again.

10 Save your work by choosing File > Save.

Tip #2: Make a Quiz

The joys of a pop quiz... hopefully making them can be as much fun as giving them. To build your quizzes quickly, you can use one of several useful templates that come with Pages.

Remember, Quizzes don't have to be teacher-created. In the classroom, having students create quizzes is a good way to get students to master the curriculum because they need to know it well enough to devise effective questions.

1   Launch Pages. The Template Chooser opens.

2   Click the Word Processing category and choose Miscellaneous, then select Quiz, and click Choose.

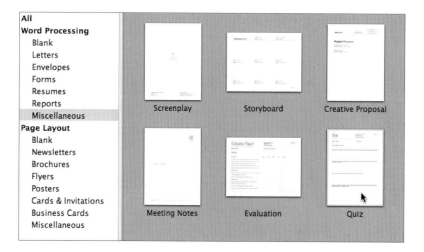

A new, untitled document opens. The first page is an essay-question–style exam.

3   Choose File > Save; name the file and store it on your local hard drive.

The quiz is ready to be modified to match the style and needs for your classroom. You need to replace the placeholder text.

4   Double-click any text block and replace the placeholder text.

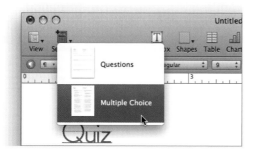

5   If you need to add more questions, click the Sections button in the toolbar and choose to add new sections. You can add a Questions or Multiple Choice style page.

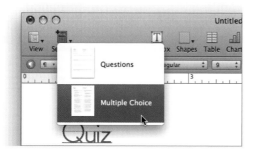

TIP ▸ If you have more than ten quiz questions, add another page by clicking the Sections button. Then open the Text Inspector and click List. Click the radio button next to Continue from previous in the Bullets & Numbering section.

6   To check the spelling of your document, choose Edit > Spelling > Spelling….

7   When ready choose File > Print and target a classroom computer for printing.

8   Save your work by choosing File > Save.

Tip #3: Create a Form Letter

How often do you need to create a form letter to send to parents? If you'd like to personalize these letters, Pages makes it easy to insert data you've defined as contacts in Address Book.

This can save you time because you can reuse a letter, permission slip, envelope, or other document for multiple people. This feature is often called a mail merge.

Several of Pages' templates contain Address Book fields. Your contact data can be automatically inserted into these fields. Students can also use this Pages feature for personalized letter-writing campaigns if they are writing about issues.

1   Launch Pages. The Template Chooser opens.

2   Click the Word Processing category, choose Letters or Envelopes, then select a style and click Choose. A new, untitled document opens.

3   Choose File > Save; name the file and store it on your local hard drive. The letter or envelope is ready to be modified for your classroom needs.

4   Pages has already inserted your contact information into the Sender fields. Your name and contact information has already been entered. Pages fills Sender fields using the Address Book card that's designated My Card.

5 Write your letter and fill in all text information as needed. The text you see onscreen is placeholder text. Simply click on a text field and start to type. When finished, you'll need to set up an address group for your students' families.

6 Launch the Address Book application by clicking its icon in the Dock.

7 Enter the contact information for your students' families. Create one card for each address.

8 Create a new group for your classroom by choosing File > New Group.

9 Drag all of your classroom cards into the group.

10 Switch back to Pages. You're ready to personalize your document for multiple recipients.

11 Choose Edit > Merge Address Book Cards.

12 Choose an Address Book group to merge from the pop-up menu.

13 Specify where to Merge Cards to: either a New Document or Send to Printer.

14 Click OK. Pages generates multiple documents, one addressed to each recipient in the Address Book group.

15 Save your work by choosing File > Save.

Tip # 4: Convert a PowerPoint Presentation

Not everyone realizes that you can export a Keynote slideshow as a PDF file or a PowerPoint file. That means you can easily share your Keynote presentations with people using other presentation applications, such as Microsoft PowerPoint, or other platforms.

Even more important, if you have old presentations that were created in PowerPoint, you can easily convert them into Keynote presentations to take advantage of the many powerful graphics and animation features in Keynote and OS X.

The conversion process from PowerPoint is relatively easy, and the vast majority of features import. Most important, the data and text are editable, so you can continue to modify your presentation in Keynote and make it more visually appealing. This is especially important for students because they are predominantly visual learners.

1   Launch Keynote. The Theme Chooser opens.

2   Click Close.

Bringing a PowerPoint presentation into Keynote allows you to modify and edit the
content. The conversion process is as easy as opening a file.

3   Choose File > Open.

4   Navigate to the PowerPoint file.

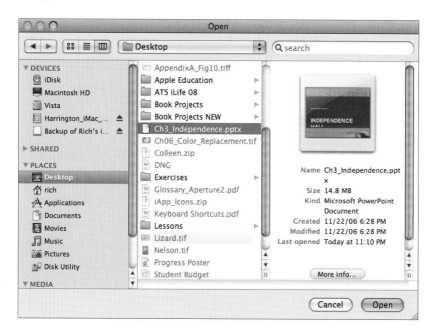

NOTE ▸ Newer Office XML formats found in PowerPoint 2007 use the extension
pptx. Keynote can open the older ppt files as well.

5   Click Open.

Keynote converts the file and gives it the same filename as the original, but adds the
.key extension. The original PowerPoint document remains unmodified on your hard
drive. A warning box informs you of any conversion errors.

6   Click Review to see any problems with conversion. Depending upon fonts loaded on your system and a few other factors, you may see a few errors. These are usually very minor and may result in slight, cosmetic changes to some of the charts.

You'll need to resize the new document to optimize it for the screen. A converted PowerPoint file is usually imported into Keynote at 720 x 540 pixels. It's better to choose a more standard resolution to match a projector.

7   Open the Document Inspector.

8   Click the Slide Size menu and choose 1024 x 768.

9   Press Command-S to save your document.

Tip #5: Make a Checklist

A checklist is a useful way to help students get organized or plan for a project. To make it easier to generate a checklist, Numbers offers an easy-to-use template.

1   Launch Numbers. The Template Chooser opens.

2   Select the Checklist template and click Choose.

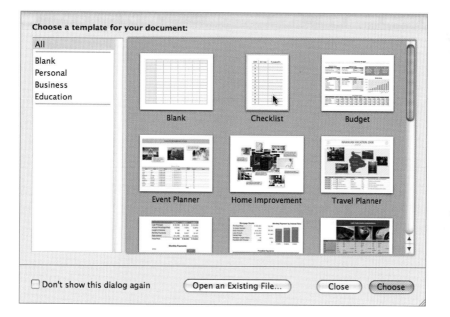

A new, untitled document opens.

3   Choose File > Save; name the file and store it on your local hard drive. The checklist is ready to be modified to match the needs for your classroom.

4   Double-click any cell and add your own text. If needed, you can add additional rows or columns using the Table menu.

5   Format text as needed using the standard features of the Format Bar.

6   Save your work by choosing File > Save.

Index

Designed to be used with *Apple Training Series:
A Teacher's Guide to Digital Media in the Classroom*,
this discounted bundle includes the following two books:

Apple Training Series: iWork '08

In the only Apple-certified book on iWork '08, your students will use Keynote, Pages, and Numbers to produce sophisticated results. Author Richard Harrington starts out with the basics of the software interface and quickly has your students designing, editing, and publishing.

This Value Pack is available from www.peachpit.com or your favorite retailer.

Apple Training Series: iLife '08

In the only Apple-certified guide to iLife '08, Michael Cohen, Jeff Bellow, and Richard Harrington will have your students working miracles with iLife within the first few pages. Focused lessons take students step by step through all aspects of iLife '08—everything from organizing and sharing photo libraries to creating polished video and soundtracks.

Other great training resources for the classroom from Peachpit include:
The Macintosh iLife 08 in the Classroom,
Jim Heid with Ted Lai
ISBN: 0-321-54926-0